# Commissioned to Heal
## and
## Other Helpful Essays

# COMMISSIONED TO HEAL
### and
# OTHER HELPFUL ESSAYS

by

## George Bennett

*Author of*

Miracle at Crowhurst
The Heart of Healing
In His Healing Steps

Published by

## ARTHUR JAMES LIMITED

THE DRIFT EVESHAM WORCS.
WR11 4NW

*First Edition 1979*

© Divine Healing Mission (Crowhurst)

Gibbons Barford Print, Wolverhampton

# PREFACE

It is a great privilege for us, as his Trustees, to write a Preface for this collection of articles by George Bennett. In his writing, as in his preaching, he had a wonderful gift of making clear the glorious truth that Jesus Christ is "the same yesterday, today, and forever", and that His healing mercies are as available to us in the twentieth century as they were in Judea in the first. His three books — *Miracle at Crowhurst, The Heart of Healing* and *In His Healing Steps* reveal the development of his personal faith and practice in the Healing Ministry.

George's death, at the age of sixty-five on Ascension Day, May 4th 1978, was a great blow to countless people. Many who now come across his books are led to discover more about this distinctive Ministry of the Church. Here are re-issued some of the articles and pamphlets which he wrote while Warden of Crowhurst, the Residential Headquarters of the Divine Healing Mission.

We gladly commend this varied anthology, compiled by Dr. Ruth Büchle, both to those who have known and loved George during his lifetime, and to those who hear of him and his work for the first time.

JACK AND JAN HEAD

Sutton
Surrey
April 1979

# CONTENTS

# 1

## COMMISSIONED TO HEAL

NO ASPECT of the Church's life and witness is more basic and central than that of her ministry of healing. This is a truth that has come back to us in the twentieth century after long years of its having almost disappeared into the shade.

This return is a phenomenon of our age and it is world-wide. It is not confined to any one church or to any one locality. Since 1953 conferences have been held biennially on an international scale for those who work whole-time or almost whole-time in this ministry. Representatives come to it from many different nations and communions and, though they speak different tongues, their language is the same. They find that their experiences are remarkably similar. The sphere of divine healing has its own laws of discipline and order.

The phenomenon is widening. More and more clergy, ministers and lay folk are being caught up in it. And once they have been, they discover a new and profound experience of the Holy Spirit. For, of course, it finds its origin in Him. The Holy Spirit is breathing this ministry back into His Church. It is not just a movement that we are trying to push, not just a legitimate concern of the Church to be placed alongside many others. Healing is not an optional extra. It is basic. It is central. It derives its authority from the lips of the Lord Himself. It is rooted in the gospel and is an integral part of it. "Preach the kingdom and heal the sick," He said. His commission is a two-fold one. Preaching and healing go hand in hand. This is the two-pronged weapon for man's redemption from the powers of evil.

When Jesus began His work of redemption He openly made a proclamation of what His life was to be all about. He went into the synagogue, took a roll of Holy Scripture and selected one particular passage from it. He found the place where it was written: "The spirit of the Lord is upon me, because he hath anointed me to preach the gospel to the poor; he hath sent me to heal the broken-hearted, to preach deliverance to the captives and recovering of sight to the blind, to set at liberty them that are bruised, to preach the acceptable year of the Lord." This was to be both the purpose and the pattern of His ministry. From then onwards, both by spoken word and by outstretched hand He began to redeem mankind from the power of the enemy and to establish His kingdom. For, since time began, man had fallen and could not return to God by his own power. Evil had entered the world and its powers had let loose the twin destroyers, sin and sickness. Man, under the Fall, was "without God, without hope, in the world."

There are none of those words, in this opening proclamation, that we have found ourselves most commonly using, like "the need for repentance". They are more gracious than that, more confident, more authoritative. They contain within themselves the seeds of His Easter victory. They are full of promise and of the living hope. There is nothing here of pharisaism in either ancient or modern form.

John the Baptist felt this difficulty. It was all so different from what he had expected. He began to have doubts about Jesus and sent a message to Him: "Art thou He that should come or do we look for another?" Consider Jesus' answer. "In that same hour He cured many of their infirmities and plagues, and of evil spirits; and unto many that were blind He gave sight. Then (the enacted reply being over) Jesus answering said unto them Go your way and tell John what things ye have seen ... And blessed is he whosoever shall not be offended in me."

Here, then, is the full gospel of our Lord, Jesus Christ. He came to lift man out of the ditch into which he had fallen. He did not stop to moralise. He did not impose conditions to be obeyed before stretching out His hands to save and to heal. If faith was there, that was all He wanted. "Jesus, son of David, have mercy upon me," pleaded Bartimaeus. "What do you want from me?" Jesus asked. "Lord, that I may receive my sight." That was all the Lord asked. In that short conversation the whole power of the gospel was let loose.

When the man sick of the palsy was brought into His presence it did not matter whether He said, "Son, thy sins be forgiven thee," or "Take up thy bed and walk." Whichever words He used or might use, the reality of His gospel of redemption was being expressed and His powers over the powers of evil were being demonstrated. He had come to set us free!

Only one real session of practical training did our Lord give to His first disciples. He might conceivably have chosen something else. The one He actually did choose was to send them forth two by two with His authority to preach the kingdom and heal the sick. And they went forth... and they healed. They were astonished at the power of His name. "Lord, even the devils are subject unto us!"

His Church was to continue His work of redemption. "As the Father hath sent me, even so send I you."

For three centuries this happened. The Church was indeed the Body of Christ. She was separate and apart from the world. There were no hazy edges round the boundary of the Christian Church. There were no half-measures. It cost something to be a Christian. Either you were or were not a member of His Church. If you were, you were committed to a saving and healing gospel. The one part was integral to the other. Preaching and healing together proclaimed the whole gospel of her Lord.

Then came the change. The emperor of the mighty

Roman empire was converted. He decreed that all his kingdom should become Christian and in the space of a short time thousands of pagans were baptised into the Church.

And, with them, their unbeliefs! Where Christ had regarded sickness as something to be rebuked, to be thrown out, it was now something to be stoically welcomed as a chastening gift from God! Where Christ had regarded a sick man as someone to be healed and released from the powers of the enemy he was now regarded as a man with a God-given opportunity to develop his spiritual life! The primitive beliefs of the Church, based squarely upon the gospel of her Lord, had now become seriously undermined by the intellectual wisdom of Graeco-Roman philosophy. A new stage had begun. The Church's concern was now to be only that of the soul. Her activity was to be confined to preaching. Half of the evangelists' records of our Lord's life was now to be ignored or, at the best, interpreted in a "spiritual" way. Miracles were out!

The Holy Spirit is calling us back today. We have got used to miracles of conversion. He is now re-acquainting us with miracles of healing. There is much in us still that has to be cleansed, to be re-awakened. But faith is returning step by step. We are being made by Him, even in this twentieth century, to enlarge our gospel, to fill it out till it contains the length and depth and breadth and height of the whole gospel which our risen Lord Himself entrusted to us.

The Church has many legitimate concerns. It is right that she address herself to every aspect of life, for all life is made by God to be redeemed by Him. We have a concern, therefore, for politics, for industry and agriculture, for medicine, for education and so on. But none of these concerns, however right and proper they may be, compare with the Church's commission to heal. All these are on the periphery of the Church's life; they are to do with the outreaches of the gospel. But healing is at the centre.

Our gospel, therefore, to industry is itself a gospel of healing. And so is our gospel to the whole of our social and political life.

An individual Christian can, conceivably, have no part in the proclamation of the gospel to industry, but no individual Christian can ignore healing as an integral part of the gospel by which, moment by moment, he lives.

A significant point to add at this juncture is that Jesus Himself refused to enter very far into discussion on questions relating to social justice and politics. He would not be drawn to make a judgment in regard to the share-out of possessions between a man and his brother and when confronted with a question of political importance His only reply was, "Render unto Caesar the things that are Caesar's but unto God the things that are God's." On the other hand, whenever and wherever anyone came to Him for healing He dealt with the matter as though it was of central, supreme and most urgent import. Not one did He refuse, turn away or ignore.

His mission was, and is, to rescue mankind from the Fall and from all its consequences, to overthrow Satan and all his works, to establish His own kingdom, to bring mankind back home to His Father, our Father.

He sends us forth to continue His work. It is His gospel we are concerned about, His work of redemption, His word of salvation from all the powers of the enemy. We are to carry the fruits of His victory over all the hosts of wickedness in high places that break down and destroy and seek the ruin of mankind. In other words, it is the risen Christ we are called to present to mankind.

This was the message of the early Church. Christ is risen! Believe and find your salvation in Him. Believe and find your healing in Him. That is the message He is giving us again in this twentieth century. It is a message about supernatural things, about the powers of a higher order

breaking through into this, it is a message about miracles.
It is epitomised in the words of Peter as he and John met a
crippled beggar at the Beautiful Gate of the temple:
"Silver and gold have I none, but that which I have, that
give I thee. In the name of Jesus, rise up and walk."

Early in my own ministry I was brought face to face
with a challenge to my belief in the power of the risen
Christ to heal. I had been converted from atheism when I
was a medical student and therefore had already
experienced His power to save, but all attempts at finding
the truth in regard to His power to heal in the Church
today had only resulted in my being handed a book by
someone or other about "the problem of suffering"! And
this with the added comment, "It's all very difficult"!

I was a curate in a very large parish in Coventry. A
sidesman of our church had become suddenly and
seriously ill with pneumonia. These were the days before
penicillin. Pneumonia was a killer then and because he
had a weak heart it was very doubtful if he would survive
the crisis. He had been ill for three days before the news
reached me.

When I knocked on the door his wife told me that two
specialists had been called in and she thought that my
knock had been that of a nurse whom they were sending.
Her husband was not to be disturbed, she told me, and she
could not, therefore, let me see him. I asked if I could go
up quietly and simply say a little prayer, but so strongly
had she been impressed that on no account was he to be
disturbed that she could not accede to my pleading.

I turned from the door with a very heavy heart, feeling
terribly frustrated, and marvelling that although sick folk
turned to Christ for His healing power in the days when
He lived amongst us in a mortal body yet His
representatives were considered in our age to be in the
way!

I walked up and down the streets of that parish for the
next hour or two, feeling desperately unable to do

anything at all. I was right in the middle of a dark wood and wondering what my ministry was all about. It was a critical time for me, too.

As I walked, three questions came into my mind. They came one after another, with an interval between each. They were as clear and as concise as can be. And, as each one came, I knew that my whole ministry from then on would be influenced by the answers I gave. There could be no equivocation.

They came "out of the blue". The first one was: "Do I really believe that when Christ was upon earth He healed people?" To this question I felt I had to give my own answer, no one else's. There came flooding back to my mind all sorts of recollections from my Theological College days, recollections of addresses I had heard, of casual but shaping conversations I had shared with my fellow students. The Modernists had much to say in those days. Do I really believe that Christ healed people when He was on earth? I had to give an answer and I gave it without qualification. But I was still in the wood and still deeply troubled.

Then came the second question. It came as suddenly as did the first. "Do I believe that after they killed Him, Christ really rose again?" It was odd, perhaps, that I had to answer this particular question. The reality of His living presence had been with me since the days of my conversion. Nevertheless, in this new situation, it seemed that I had to answer it all over again. I gave my answer.

Then came the third question. It came quite soon after I had answered the second. There was not such a long gap this time. "Do I really believe that Christ is the same yesterday, today and for ever?" With this question came my final wrestling. It took a few minutes and then I gave my reply.

It was as though I had come home. I had left the wood behind. A tremendous sense of peace flooded over me.

I look back to this experience as the decisive point in

my ministry. It was not so much a turning point as one in which a number of previous dimly perceived beliefs and earlier partial experiences of the Lord's healing power suddenly came into sharp focus. I look back to it as to a point in my journey beyond which I could never afterwards return. It was, for me, an experience of existential importance.

What happened afterwards, though wonderful in itself, was no more than the confirmation of it, though it did set the seal to it.

I returned to the sick man's house — I suppose it must have been a couple of hours later — was admitted by his wife and made my way upstairs. Long years after, I asked her if I had been rude in pushing past her. She told me that that wasn't so. Some force had made her accept the situation. His room was in semi-darkness. The curtains had been partially drawn to keep out the glare of a bright sunny day. Yet the whole room seemed to me to be full of the power of the risen Christ. I knew nothing in those days about the laying-on-of-hands and I knelt simply at his bedside. Instinctively, I felt that I must touch him. At that moment he raised his hand under the coverlet and I took it in mine. The prayer I said was very simple. Any child could have said it. But it seemed important that a prayer be said while I held him. As though the prayer and the touch were like a switch that could turn on the light! The power was there but needed to be conveyed to him! As I rose to go he said, "Thank you! I'll be all right now. You will tell my wife, won't you?" She was still standing in the hall. I gave her his message and went out into the sunshine.

Fifteen years later I returned to Coventry and joined the staff at the Cathedral. I was "in residence" each Monday. This day, at least, became a day on which sick folk looked to the Cathedral to find not only their Saviour but their healing Lord too. On the first Monday of each month we would hold a Service of Healing in the Chapel of Unity and this man was its most frequent attender and one of my most faithful supporters and intercessors.

Through the years one has seen the healing power of the risen Christ at work in the lives of hundreds of people, and one has seen a tremendous growth in the number of circles that offer intercessory prayer for healing of the sick. And one has seen His answers! He seems to make His presence more real to one in the carrying out of this His work than in any other aspect of our ministry.

I believe that this fuller understanding of the gospel is being outpoured upon us by the Holy Spirit today and that when the whole Church of Christ has accepted it we shall look back on our present understandings of it as being cluttered up with a whole lot of beliefs that derive their origin not from the New Testament but from man's wisdom. I believe that this fuller understanding of the gospel is the gospel of the future as it was of the Early Church. It contains within itself the living seeds of a new revival.

I believe, also, that this is the catalyst which will draw the broken parts of Christ's Body, the Church, together again. However hard we struggle along the ecumenical line, however many thousands of discussions we have about either faith or order, we shall not come together until this new, yet old, conception has been gladly welcomed back.

I believe that its acceptance is what the Holy Spirit is forcing upon His whole Church throughout the world in these climacteric days as perhaps His final gift before there comes the consummation of the age and the great Day which now begins to draw nigh.

# 2

## OBEDIENCE TO THE
## HOLY SPIRIT

THE LORD is good to us, abundantly merciful. And we bow our heads in gratitude to Him. He blesses the work.

It is because this work is, and must be, the work of the Holy Spirit that I rebel whenever I hear anyone say that healing should follow certain lines, a certain pattern. The truth is that we just don't know beforehand how the Holy Spirit is going to guide, dictate and control. Every individual is an individual. He cannot be made to conform to a pattern.

Healing work is to do with our obedience to the dictation of the Holy Spirit and not to a pre-arranged and pre-decided set of formulae.

There are many ways in which, and through which, the healing forces flow. To us who are concerned with the Church's ministry of healing they are as many as there are persons who come or write to us for help. For us in the Divine Healing Mission these number hundreds every week. Each one is an individual. To each one, the risen Lord has a special word. We cannot make them all conform to one pre-set pattern.

Yet there are certain "tools" He has given us to use. They are there to take and use *but only at His bidding*. These include confession and absolution, with or without penance, holy unction, the laying-on-of-hands, exorcism, the prayer of faith, the Holy Communion, the reading of His Word, and so on. All these carry the divine forces of healing and all are intended for our use. *But only at His bidding*. It is a matter of obedience to His direction if they are used at all.

Every ministrant or healer finds through experience the

way in which the Holy Spirit intends him to work. His way may not be the way of others. What I say now, therefore, is put forward, humbly and necessarily briefly, as an explanation of how one such ministrant works. It may help some of the clergy and ministers who read this.

An interview with a sufferer usually lasts from half to three-quarters of an hour. From the very outset the ministrant must enter into a two-way conversation. On the one hand there is the conversation with the risen Lord (or, if it comes easier that way, with the Holy Spirit). This is as important as the other conversation, i.e. with the sufferer.

By the word conversation I mean something deeper than the mere words spoken. It has to do with a traffic of the soul. The conversation with the sufferer starts quite simply but then develops gradually until the sufferer's life has been laid before one. But every step is determined by that other conversation, the conversation with the Unseen.

How often, during the course of these interviews one has been given to say something to the sufferer that has had nothing whatever to do with the surface conversation of the spoken word, and which has put a finger right on the root of the malaise!

All that the ministrant can do is to act as a link between the sufferer and the source of his ultimate healing, our blessed Lord, Jesus Christ.

At the end of the interview, there usually comes a silence. It is something like one of those silences that occasionally happen in large dining-rooms. All has been said. There is a lapse. It is then that the conversation on the human side — with the sufferer — is suspended temporarily while the ministrant waits on the Lord's bidding.

All of this has been put very quickly but I have written it only to make my point about the importance of letting the Holy Spirit do His work in His own way and to show that obedience is the most important thing so far as we are concerned.

Out of this continuing experience in the healing work of the Church one feels there are only two necessities in the attitude of the sufferer which must be in him by the end of the interview, if healing is to follow.

They are (1) expectant faith and (2) total surrender.

The expectant faith is a faith born of, or confirmed by, the Spirit during the interview. Any previous faith that the sufferer may have had will now be swallowed up into a larger faith. For instance, before he came, he may have had a kind of faith in the ability of "the healer" to cure his bad leg. He now has the larger faith that sees only Christ as the Healer, and the Healer not simply of his bad leg but of all of him, his fears, his emotional illnesses, his selfishness, and so on. He came to look for a little thing. He thought it was the most important thing in the world. He is "sorted out" now, he has got things into their proper perspective. His whole expectation is enlarged.

Total surrender is the second necessity, the second step. As he kneels to receive the ministration the healer is told to give him, his soul and mind are wide open. An hour ago he could never have had the slightest notion of how he would be now.

In that state and at that moment a healing blessing is given him. Certainly he will go away a different person. He may, or may not, find his bad leg easier. Very often, he will. But he will know that the risen Christ has touched his life. And that brings me to say one more thing about this obedience we must have.

What happens beyond the interview is not our concern. Not, that is, so far as results are concerned. We have done what we have been required to do. It is all, now in the Lord's hands.

As the sufferer leaves us we must give thanks for having been allowed to do this work for him, we must give thanks that the Lord has blessed him according to His own dear will. And that is always far better than our desires, however holy, however compassionate, however good.

## 3

# THE MINISTRY OF LISTENING

THE MOST IMPORTANT thing in the practice of the ministry of healing is listening to people as they tell of their troubles. Listening and sharing! Having a "healing touch" in one's hands matters very little without this.

Some folk desire the gift of healing and perhaps even pray for it. What they have in mind is a miracle touch which will relieve pain and restore physical health. But there's much more to it than that. The gifts of the Holy Spirit are outlined in I Corinthians, 12. If you read this chapter carefully and thoughtfully you will notice that whereas all the other gifts mentioned are put in the singular, this is the only one spoken of in the plural. St. Paul speaks of the gifts of healing, not of the gift.

By using the plural, I think he intends us to understand that the ministry of healing embraces a wide variety of approaches. Besides the laying-on-of-hands there is holy unction, Confession, Prayer (specially Intercessory or "Absent"), and so on. The service of Holy Communion is a great Service of Healing. In the Invitation I often add the words "...and healing" to "...and take this Holy Sacrament to your comfort..." They seem to be most appropriate at this point and help to draw out the healing content of the blessed sacrament which might otherwise stay unappropriated. So it is "the gifts of healing" — in the plural — that we are concerned about and not just a "gift of healing" confined to a physical touch.

Listening and sharing — that is the main thing about the Church's ministry of healing. And perhaps it is the most important of all the gifts of healing! To listen means listening with one's heart as well as with one's ears. It means feeling the hurts that the sufferer is feeling. For hurts make a sufferer feel isolated. And this, not only from his normal good health but also from the fellowship of others. Hurts cut him off from life and the first thing he needs is the companionship of some other person who is patient enough to share the feeling of his hurts with him, someone who can help share the load, someone who can understand how he feels. This is the beginning of healing.

Hundreds of times one has just sat down with a sufferer and let him talk. Often, one discovers, it is the first time in his life he has been able to unburden himself like this! When he has finished speaking one has taken him in prayer to the Lord and then ministered to him. The prayer and the ministration have been important, of course, perhaps vital, but I can't help thinking they would not have meant half so much to him had there not been the long outpouring of his troubles first.

Though I have listened to the stories of hundreds of sufferers it still leaves me with a sense of wonder that just sitting and listening can have such a potent effect in their healing. In the talks we have had together — though I personally say very little — one feels quite clearly a movement of the spirit taking place. I ought perhaps to say, of the Holy Spirit. For certainly, as one listens, one feels not only the hurts which the sufferer himself is feeling but also something of the compassion of Christ the great Healer of us all. One feels the movement of the burden being lifted and then transferred to Him who bears all our sufferings. One doesn't necessarily talk about these things during the conversation. I don't think there is a need to. The sufferer feels it himself and doesn't need words of explanation. No two sufferers are exactly alike — there may be similarities, here and there, to others — each one is different. The burdens of each one are unique. This is probably why one feels this sense of wonder afresh each time.

To listen to a person, accepting him just as he is, to enter into a spiritual bond with him, to converse with him at a level which is even deeper than the actual words you speak, to feel his troubles in your own person as though they were your own, to share with him the burden of his suffering so that he is no longer alone, to accompany him as he searches so hard for the right way forward — this, surely, is the one essential in all the gifts of healing.

Listening to people! If we get this right in our thinking we shall be the better able to see and understand that the ministry of healing is not an optional extra to the Gospel, something added on. We shall begin to see that the ministry of healing in the Church is absolutely fundamental and inescapable.

During the Lenten season we think of how our Lord came among us to share with us the burdens we have to carry and the hurts that come our way. He was lovingly and obediently content to take our sins and our sufferings into Himself. It is by His stripes we are healed. This same task He commits to His Church, to all who follow Him.

We are instructed to bear one another's burdens, to confess our sins one to another. Do we ever do this? Dare we ever do this? Look around any Christian congregation and you will see a lot of lonely people. Many of them are carrying hurts, some long buried and festering deep down, who never even thought of healing being possible for them.

We are too suspicious of each other! It would never do for the person who sits next to me in the pew every Sunday to know of the hurt I've been suffering through these years and my seeming failure to find the right answer in dealing with it! And I would have to think twice about telling my vicar or minister about it! Whatever would he think if he knew? Lord, save us! How we perish in our blindness and unfaith! How can we go on refusing to accept Your gifts?

People get shut in with their hurts. They don't know

what to do with them. They don't know anyone they can go to who will listen and "understand". Yet this is the heart of our healing ministry.

Yet the people who have helped me most in my own life and whom I will forever remember with gratitude to God are those who have listened to me — hardly making a spoken comment — while I have poured out my problem to them. The pity is that there are so few. Most folk want to give advice.

Helping (or healing) a person in this way should not be regarded as an "opportunity". This word is used far too often! I am thinking particularly of the many times I've heard it from the lips of those earnest young Christians of all ages who seem to spend their lives looking round for opportunities to serve the Lord!

I love that old story of St Francis of Assisi which goes something like this. One of his earnest young followers, eagerly looking for opportunities to serve the Lord, was invited by St Francis to accompany him on a journey round the neighbouring villages. On their arrival at the first village they reached the market place where he thought there would be a good opportunity of preaching the gospel. But nothing seemed to happen. St Francis didn't preach nor did the saint ask him to. All they did was to stay for a little while chatting with folk here and there. They then went on to the next village where the same thing happened. And so they travelled, through village after village, till they returned home. The young follower felt very frustrated and depressed. He could not stop himself from asking St Francis why he had not used the many opportunities offered him. They could have preached the gospel in many market places that day! But hadn't they been doing just that, St Francis asked him, while they were walking and talking with friends they had met on the way?

We don't have to look for opportunities and we certainly don't have to create them. They just happen day by day. And when they do happen it is best if we don't recognise them as such! Jesus never used the occasion of someone coming to Him in trouble as an opportunity to preach the gospel. He met them at the point of their need. Bartimaeus interrupted the important and critical journey Jesus was making to Jerusalem. "Jesus, son of David, have mercy on me," he shouted. Jesus halted, called him to His side and asked him what he wanted. In compassion, Jesus gave it to him. There was no hint of this being an "opportunity". There was no "preaching of the gospel" — which is why, strangely enough, the gospel was preached!

The next thing I want to say about this ministry of healing is that the more one goes on in it, listening to the stories of hundreds of folk, the more one is convinced that the majority of our physical illnesses spring from within. They are the deposits in the physical realm of our being of hurts that have been suffered by our inner being — our inner selves, our egos. Agnes Sanford calls the body the shock-absorber. It is as though the inner being reaches a point in its suffering when it says to the body, "I've had enough! I can't bear any more! You take over."

Time and again one has observed how a particular physical illness has been preceded by a disposition of the inner self similar to that which others suffering from the same illness have suffered. It seems as though a hurt in which one particular emotion has got out of hand (and been repressed) gives rise, in course of time, to its own particular range of physical trouble. So much so that when one is confronted by a particular form of physical illness one can almost "guess" what is going to be said in the interview about the spiritual or emotional hurt that preceded it.

The root of many a physical illness, I am sure, lies not in the body but in the inner self. Yet it isn't quite so straightforward as that. It isn't so much the hurt experienced by the sufferer that matters but rather the

response he has made to it. How did he cope with it? Did
his emotions get out of hand? It is the response that
matters, that is decisive for his health. Was his response
one of anger, resentment, self-pity? Was he bowled over
by a grief he could not bring himself to share with
anybody?

Human beings don't react. That is a word for machines.
To react means that there is no choice in the matter.
Human beings can choose. They respond. And their
response might be positive and good or negative and
harmful. When hurts come to us, therefore, and come
they most surely will, the important thing is to have the
capacity of making the right response. This is a thing that
doesn't come suddenly. It has to do with faith and the
daily disciplining of one's thoughts and emotions.

It is no use our trying to resist some of the experiences
that come our way, trying to fight them or running away.
Somehow they have to be met, accepted and absorbed. If
we meet them negatively — as, for instance, by being
filled with resentment — we are allowing the hurts to take
control and let loose within us their own particular
poisons.

Somehow, sooner or later, we have to learn the way of
LOVE. I put that in capital letters because our ordinary
human love isn't big enough. Sooner or later we have to
learn that there are really no such things as "good" and
"bad" experiences. Both kinds are needful for us and
therefore both are good. If we are ultimately to reach that
perfection which the Father has for every one of us then
we have somehow to accept all that comes, of "good" and
"ill" as within His purposes.

If you want to know the way of Love there is only one
direction to which I can point you. To the Christ upon His
Cross! He loved and went on loving, no matter what came
to Him. Somehow we have to learn how to take up *our*
cross. To carry it and fill it with Love. Not to refuse it by
being resentful about it, by fighting it, by trying to run

away from it. This way isn't easy. That is why we need each other's help. So we get back to the ministry of listening and realise again how important a part it is of the whole ministry of healing.

It is healing at a deep level that people really need, and this is what the gospel of the Kingdom is all about. This is the kind of healing that Christ was concerned about and which is inherent in His two-fold commission: "preach the Kingdom and heal the sick." But, for the most part, folk think that healing is simply glossing over the top!

They take pills and medicines thinking these will heal them, but all that pills and medicines can do is to cure the physicalised deposit of the real illness within. They can ease only the symptoms. Only One can really heal through and through. And He needs people to do His work. He needs people who will listen and share and feel and help to carry the burden, and so begin to point the way towards Him in whom, and in whom alone, the right response to every experience that comes to men can be found.

## 4

## HEALING IS A FRUIT
## OF CHRIST'S VICTORY

I WAS IMPRESSED again by this great message after
having read the New English Bible. I hope, incidentally,
that you have been able to get a copy. My own
hesitancies about it were completely overcome as
soon as I had read through St Mark's Gospel on the first
evening after its arrival. It was confirmed as I read
through the others later.

It always astonishes me that anyone can read through
one of these "lives of our Lord" and still wonder, at the
end, if healing has anything to do with the Gospel! What
also astonishes me is how full of healing it actually is. Our
Blessed Lord spent so very much of His time just healing
people. His compassion and love for all simply let loose
the healing power out of Him. It happened wherever He
went. He loved to deliver folk from the power of sickness.

And through every healing miracle you can see — can't
you?—the sign it was of His utter mastery over the powers
of evil. He was not just being kind. Not just being
compassionate. He was all of that, it is true, but mark the
deeper issues. He wrestled against "spiritual wickedness in
high places." His gentleness and loving concern masked
the grim battle beneath. His was, for all our sakes, the
final battle against our enemy. It came to its climax on
Good Friday. By Easter the victory for all time had been
won.

Don't leave the fruits of His victory on one side as
though they had never been! Don't go to a sick person, or
pray for one, just in the hope that he might be comforted
or strengthened to bear his illness. You don't go to a
sinner to give him comfort enough to be able to continue

in sin! It is his release you are after, release for Christ's sake, and in the power of His victory.

I am sure that this fuller Gospel is spreading throughout Christendom and I have a strong feeling that it will prove, when fully accepted by the whole Church, to be the opening of the door which admits the Holy Spirit fully into the revival which has already begun. I liken the rediscovery of the healing ministry of Christ in His Church to the great revival movements that have swept through the Church from time to time in the past. But, this time, it will be on a twentieth-century world scale. It will affect every aspect of the Church's thinking, worship and action. It will put completely out of date many of the books now reckoned as "musts" for those who study theology.

I feel, also, that this rediscovery will prove to be the catalyst in the many hopes for re-union that are taking shape today. When the various parts of the Broken Body accept this fuller Gospel it will be impossible for them to remain divided and apart.

And I believe that when the whole Body of Christ upon earth has accepted it we shall see His healing power much more fully at work than it is now. At the moment His healing work is incomplete, not because His victory has become less or His power waned, but because His Body upon earth is divided and, further, because each part of it is torn between faith and distrust.

But what we are given to see is sufficient and more than sufficient. Even in our tiny organisation — world-wide as it is and growing apace in its number of supporters and friends every day, it is still tiny when compared with the total number of our Christian brothers and sisters — we see clearly every day the healing powers of the risen Christ at work among us. These signs are sufficient to remove all doubt as to the full nature of His Easter victory and they point to what might and — please God — will be. The Master promised (and never once have His promises failed) that "greater works than these shall ye do because I go to the Father."

Whitsuntide is the festival of the Holy Spirit's outpouring upon the Church, Christ's Body on earth. It hasn't, as yet, the same prominence in our minds as have the festivals of Christmas and Easter. But it is gradually becoming more significant and meaningful. When the healing ministry of our blessed Lord in and through His Church is fully accepted it will engage the attention of our hearts and minds as fully as do the other festivals. There would be no such thing as a "Pentecostal Church" were the whole Church as much Pentecostal as Christmas and Easter-minded.

We have made the Christian Year an unbalanced thing. We emphasize parts of it and neglect others. We've got it out of perspective. If any period should stand out it is the great Forty Days from Easter to Ascension Day. And then we should really be prepared for the following days of waiting for the Holy Spirit's outpouring which we keep in festival on Whitsunday.

I always think the laying-on-of-hands brings a realisation of Pentecost home to us. Each laying-on-of-hands is a personal experience of it. As we kneel to receive the inflow of the Holy Spirit through this Christ-ordained act we feel and know for ourselves what Pentecost means. And we can imagine what it will mean when all our churches embrace Services of Healing into their programmes.

There is a long way yet to go. There lies much hard work ahead for each one of us. But we can take heart and give thanks for the expansion of this fuller realisation which is *already taking place*. It derives its origin and its impetus from the Holy Spirit. We give thanks to Him for what He has so far allowed us to see. And we know this is only the beginning.

## 5

# LAY HANDS ON THE SICK

TO LAY HANDS on the sick is one of the highest privileges of our ministry. It is an action which conveys the whole power of the Gospel in a way that the spoken word cannot do. For myself, I should feel a tremendous sense of frustration were my own ministry to be restricted to the voice alone.

We often sing a hymn that has the words "that my whole being may proclaim Thy Being and Thy Ways". How true! Our Gospel cannot be proclaimed and its power conveyed by the lips alone. Our whole being is needed. The hands and the eyes, as well as the lips, have to be used and dedicated in the service of the Gospel. Too often does the Church give the impression that she is all mouth, all talk. Yet the typical response of our blessed Lord to a sick man was to use His hand. It was through His touch that power was conveyed. When He spoke, the words He used were additional to and in support of the main act. They were used to encourage, to explain, to caution or to teach. When He sent His disciples out in His name He didn't tell them just to preach the Gospel but to proclaim the Gospel by preaching the kingdom and healing the sick. Both voice and touch were needed.

When confronted by a sick person one uses one's voice, of course. One sits down with him, listens to his story, says a word or two here and there as the Holy Spirit directs. One enters into a conversation with him that is deeper than the words themselves. The problem, with all its hurts, is shared. All of this is essential and inescapable. Yet, sooner or later, one reaches the limit of what words can do. It is at this point that the real challenge comes, at this point that the vital moment has arrived. One can either say goodbye with a "God bless you" or one can take the whole burden to the Lord as one gives the laying-on-of-hands and so lift the whole situation into an entirely different sphere where healing grace is let loose from on high.

It is at this point that something happens which is beyond words to express, impossible for the spoken words only to convey. In this act the Lord Himself takes over. It is He and only He who now speaks directly to the heart of the sufferer and his need. One stands apart, so to speak, from the mystery of what is happening now. One is only allowed to witness the strong power of the Lord present to heal.

Sometimes folk talk about preparing people to receive the laying-on-of-hands. It just does not work out that way. You just don't know what to prepare them for! Anything can happen! All you can say to them when the point has been reached when the laying-on-of-hands is about to be given is "Think not so much about your healing any more, about what you want of the Lord, but think only of Him and be prepared to accept whatever He wants to give." Certainly there is no formula for preparation, and if preparation is to be thought of at all it has to be thought of as something which is really the responsibility of the ministrant rather than of the sufferer.

Nor is there any special order of service — except, of course, for a public Service of Healing. Each ministrant has to say and do as he himself personally is led. The laying-on-of-hands should come "naturally" as the interview draws to a close. It would perhaps be preceded by a short time of silence in which both ministrant and sufferer wait on the Lord. During this time the ministrant will be moved to utter a spoken prayer. The Spirit will direct the thoughts of his heart and mind and perhaps will shape some of the phrases or sentences he uses. Then he commits this act for the Christ Himself to use.

As he lays his hands on the head of the sufferer he may say words such as these: "The healing mercies of the risen Lord Jesus Christ enter into your soul, your mind, your body and heal you from all that harms you, and give you His peace." No other prayer need be said. The sufferer can then be left alone with the Lord. This is a time when "He must increase and I" — be quite forgotten!

In these days when the Holy Spirit is pouring Himself afresh upon the Church we rejoice to see some of His distinctive gifts returning, and many clergy and ministers are feeling His presence more and more when visiting the sick. Those of us who are ordained simply must go forward in this matter. We must overcome the negative indoctrinations we received at our theological colleges. We have to break through our hesitations about entering into a dangerous and suspect sphere, about raising false hopes that might destroy the sufferer's faith, about seeming to suggest some sort of magic.

Most of us, if we stop to think for a moment, have had some experience of the Lord's healing power through our ministry. What about that child we were called out to christen because he was unlikely to survive the night, and immediately afterwards took a turn for the better? And what about that member of your congregation who recovered following your visit or the prayers of your people? The Lord really does scatter hints about our path if only we have eyes to see them!

It isn't by any means essential that a parson has to have the charismatic gifts of Healing before he can do anything. Surely He has made that quite plain. The rubric in the Prayer Book about the condition of the celebrant at Holy Communion is a fair enough guide for that. It just isn't good enough to shirk one's responsibility in this matter by saying that one hasn't been given a charismatic gift like the parson in the next parish! By virtue of our ordination we must proclaim, be the channels of, the Gospel with every part of our being. We are set apart and called to preach the Gospel and heal the sick in our Master's name. His is the gift, not ours.

The results, too, are in His hands. The same truth applies to our preaching and to every other part of our ministry. To the best of our ability we can present to our people the challenge of the Gospel from our pulpits, but the results are His, not ours. And even if we preached a thousand such sermons and nothing happened, nobody responded, we should still have to go on preaching the Kingdom. If we were as concerned about results following our preaching as perhaps we are about the laying-on-of-hands we should probably not go into the pulpit again. And that might not be such a bad idea, either!

What happens is His concern, not ours. Time and again one has stood at the altar immediately before giving the laying-on-of-hands, feeling a complete sense of inadequacy and unworthiness — sometimes even to the point of a devastating hopelessness — when one has seemed to hear the Lord saying, "All I want you to do is to put your hands on these poeple and say a few words — that is all. I will give the power." And He has always kept His promise!

Are folk suddenly healed? Well, they often are. But I think there is a misconception in this question. It isn't that some strange power gives a kind of magic touch. It is more to do with a flow of healing grace. Certainly, what happens in that moment is sudden, just as in the same way you may be suddenly aware of a movement of the Holy Spirit touching you, or as in a moment of sudden insight into the mysteries of God. You can't explain these things in ordinary human language. But you know that something has suddenly happened and you are that much different now from what you were before it happened. Grace has come into you.

So with a healing ministration. Through this act there is a movement of the Spirit. Healing grace is given. What the results will be are not the ministrant's concern. He stands by, he witnesses the supernatural grace of God breaking through into this natural human frame, his spirit is filled with wonder.

The sufferer may sometimes try to describe what has happened. The fact that the pain or the disability is gone seems to be no longer of major importance to him. All this has been swallowed up by a greater experience. There is a glow in his eyes as he speaks. His talk is of God's glory.

Though one has seen His healing power at work in the lives of all kinds of physical and mental suffering and therefore has learned to rule out nothing as impossible with God, one is also reminded of those folk who, though not having been completely healed of their illness, yet have been absolutely and completely filled with the knowledge of His healing grace at work in them. I am thinking now of a young woman who died from cancer a year ago. She should (medically speaking) have died much earlier and suffered physically much more than she did. Undoubtedly the Lord blessed her through the laying-on-of-hands and in the extra two or three years that He gave her she was used mightily as a channel of His grace. She became radiant. One day, when the end was in sight, she told me, "I wouldn't have missed this for the world. I have been a member of a prayer group for years and have joined in prayer for the healing of hundreds of sick folk. But now, to be on the receiving end of prayer and ministration is beyond anything that words can express." There was a lovely light in her eyes. The light of Christ. She was experiencing something that was not of this world. Already she was "in paradise".

Though Christ's healing power through His Church is not dependent on the ministrant having a healing gift, we do *hope to* recognise that healing gifts exist. St Paul's great chapter (Romans xii) on the gifts of the Spirit is coming alive to our generation in a new way. These are called "charismatic" because they are gifts given by the Holy Spirit "by Grace", but that doesn't mean they are scattered at random here and there like leaflets from an aeroplane. Gifts have to be cultivated and exercised if they are to grow. It isn't that someone wakes up in the morning to find he has suddenly and miraculously been given the gift of preaching, the gift of administration, the gift of healing or any other gift, and until that happens he mustn't do a thing. Yet that is sometimes the impression given.

A year or two ago a friend of mine, a supporter of the D.H.M. and frequent contributor to *The Healer,* produced a little book about the Lord's healing work. One review began with words something like this: "It is not the first time we have heard of a clergyman with a charismatic gift." Cruel words to use, inferring that it could be therefore dismissed by most of its readers. The view correlates the charismatic gift with magic.

There are two ways in which the healing gift may come. The first is seen in those who seem to have a natural gift. They are born with "healing hands". The other, and the one with which we are more concerned, comes through prayerful obedience and practice. When a parson first gives the laying-on-of-hands it is more or less just a symbolic gesture. He will probably feel a little selfconscious about it and will give it while a whole range of doubts flit across his mind. But he will give it none-the-less and chiefly as a symbol of compassion and blessing. The likelihood is that at this early stage he will not be conscious of any "flow of power"; but that will come. Learning any art is difficult. It takes ages to get the "feel" of it and it is easy enough to become discouraged. But as you go on steadily and patiently, the "feel" of it comes. You know that a new door is opened and that tremendous possibilities lie ahead.

I often think that in this matter of a charismatic gift the teaching of our Lord about "to him that hath shall be given and from him that hath not shall be taken away even that which he hath" is very pertinent.

As he goes on he finds that his touch becomes sensitive to pain (he feels a heat vibration in its locality), to tense parts of the body and to locked joints. He suddenly senses a "vibration" of power coming through. Instinctively he goes to the spot where the trouble is and he knows just how long to hold his hands there and when to take them away. These are just a few of the "outward" experiences he discovers. But, more wonderful still, the reality of heaven, of the spiritual world, of the communion of saints, of the support of holy angels, and chiefly of the presence of the risen Christ bursts vividly upon his consciousness in a way that far surpasses his experiences when, in the old days, he was only preaching. And his people too, are finding the glory of Christ through this ministry far more widely and more deeply than they could ever possibly have done when the gospel was limited in its proclamation to speech alone.

# 6

## GOD'S WHOLE CREATION

THERE ARE TWO questions I am sometimes asked about animals. One is about their response to the laying-on-of-hands and the other is whether or not they go to Paradise. They do, indeed, respond. Sometimes, I have done this for them and I know that others have. Among other things, one has seen tumours lose their malignancy and cease growing. Obviously, this is done quietly and without formality and usually in silence. The lovely thing is that the animal seems to know something of what is happening. Your pets know and trust you, so simply put your hands on the afflicted part and lift your heart lovingly to the Father, rebuke the illness in His Name and then let His Love pour through you and into your pet.

Is there a place for them in Paradise? The "quick" answer, and I am sure also (when all the theological implications have been discussed) the truest final answer is Yes.

While thinking of the "whole creation" one ought to add a few words about plant life. At certain times of the year the Church has festivals which are concerned with Nature, Plough Sunday, Rogation Days, Harvest Thanksgiving. I am absolutely certain that these are not just motivated by mere sentimentality or anything like that. I believe that were we to understand all that there is to know about prayer we should know for certain that loving prayer "scientifically" operates on plant life, as on all life. Experiments have been carried out along these lines with tremendously interesting results, I know, but I hesitate to say more than that about them because one has a natural repugnance to anything which savours of a *testing* of prayer.

Three things come to mind concerning the last two or three paragraphs:

1. About the response of faith in the Lord's (and His Church's) healing works. While faith is an essential pre-requisite the onus is clearly not on the recipient, but on the evocator. The animal is not mustering all its resources of faith and neither is the plant. But a response of some kind seems to be evoked. The animal is clearly sensitive to "atmosphere". But it is the faith of the ministrant offered to God that is the "substance of things hoped for." Thus it was because He was what He was that Christ could evoke faith. The inference concerning the Church and especially those of us who are called to be clergy and ministers is obvious and needs no labouring.

2. The sacraments: I believe that when we bless the water and consecrate the bread and wine we are taking part in an act of far deeper significance than we shall ever be able to understand with our inhibited finite minds. To think of them simply as symbols is far too superficial and materialistic. The best we can say of any definition, even the Prayer Book one, is that it is no more than a poor pointer directing us towards what a sacrament really is.

3. The cursing of the fig tree. Most people take this to be an enacted parable. Though much can be gained from the interpretations given, I always feel that such interpretations are evasive of the real issue. They seem to be apologising for the fact that our Lord plainly did kill the fig tree by cursing it.

In my own reading of this incident I see the Lord clearly demonstrating to His disciples what the power to bless and to heal can do when reversed. It occurs right at the end of His teaching (both by demonstration and by word). He has used this power to heal many and He has already sent them out on a training mission of healing in His name. Now, He says to them in effect, suppose this same power is used to curse instead of to bless, what happens?

We don't have to search very far in our experiences of people, of families and homes, to realise what a curse can do. In the experiments on plants carried out in America and in England some seeds were blessed, others cursed. The incident of the fig tree will tell you what happened to the unfortunate seeds chosen to be cursed! Look again at the New Testament (and also the Old) and especially at the Acts of the Apostles, and the incident of the fig tree will then appear to be more than just an "enacted parable".

This, I think gives us an insight into our Lord's rebuking of the fever, of our rebuking pain in His name today.

It also gives us a clearer insight into the meaning of the sacraments, indeed of the whole nature of the Church, into what happens when a Bishop or a loaf of bread is consecrated.

When we are looking forward to the season of Advent and Christmas, we shall be thinking of such phrases as "your redemption draweth nigh". Try to see this phrase as being concerned with the ultimate redemption of God's whole creation and not only that of man. True, man is at the centre, he is the king-pin. But see him, not in isolation, but as having all the world of nature bound inseparably together with him, both in "the fall" and also in the enfolding of God's most perfect and ultimate will. Maranatha! God bless you.

## 7

## "BRING HIM TO ME!"

*Based on St. Mark, chapter 10, verses 46-52*

HERE WE HAVE, in the story of the healing of blind Bartimaeus, what appears to be a witness to the healing mercies of Jesus given by the man himself to the Evangelist St Mark when he comes to write his Gospel. It appears to be an insertion into the text which Mark wanted particularly to record. The story ends with the words, "He followed Him in the way." It may well have been that in the early Church of Jerusalem Mark met Bartimaeus and was deeply impressed by this personal witness that he made.

Try to picture the scene, therefore, from the point of view of this poor man. There were many such in the land at that time. Some were blind, some were deaf and dumb, some had leprosy, but whatever their illnesses might be, they were a liability on society. They had no jobs, were very poor and earned their daily bread by begging. Bartimaeus, therefore, was one of a great company of people.

One day, when sitting at the roadside, he hears a large number of people coming that way and something within him seems to tell him that this is not an ordinary gathering of people. He asks a passer-by about it and is told that Jesus of Nazareth is coming that way, and immediately he cries out for help.

In that moment of appealing for the help of Jesus many thoughts must have flooded his mind. He must have heard something about Jesus and we can well imagine that what he had heard had seemed to him to be truly wonderful and perhaps more wonderful than he could take in. He had heard of so many lovely miracles of healing that Jesus had wrought in the lives of poor people like himself.

He was probably not a particularly good man, nor, for that matter, a bad man — just an ordinary outcast. He probably had respect for his religion, but somehow had never found that religion as it had been shown to him really touched his deepest needs. He knew that he had a duty to God in worshipping Him and in serving Him day by day. All of these things his religious leaders had taught him. But Jesus was somehow different from them. While Jesus also taught that man had his duty to God, yet at the same time He spoke much more fully than they had ever heard before of the *love* of God for mankind, and not only for mankind but also for each individual man and woman with his or her own particular needs. There was something in Jesus which stirred the spirits of people, that was so different from the kind of religion that he had encountered so far.

And suddenly he felt at that moment, as Jesus passed on His way to Jerusalem, that this might be the most important moment of his life. He was not going to let it pass and he shouted out loud "Jesus of Nazareth, Thou Son of David, have mercy on me."

The outward needs of this poor blind man were obvious to everybody, but it was his deeper need that he suddenly wanted to bring to Jesus. As he shouted, the folk about him thought that he wanted from Jesus the kind of surface help that others occasionally gave him. They did not know that even to think about Jesus touched the inner springs of the heart. Certainly it was the deeper need that suddenly was uppermost in his mind as he cried out for help. He remembers later, when recalling the incident to St Mark, that he thrust aside his outer garment; it was as though he instinctively knew that Jesus could look right into the very core of his heart and inner being.

Jesus hears his call and halts in His stride. He tells those about Him to fetch Bartimaeus. They fetch him. Jesus says to him, "What do you want me to do for you?" and the blind man says simply, "Rabboni (dear Lord), that I may receive my sight." Jesus heals him. His deeper need is touched and fully met. From now on he need no longer sit by the wayside begging.

Here in this actual incident we have perhaps a picture of so many, hoping with only a forlorn hope that someone like Jesus will come their way. Jesus does indeed come their way, but not any longer as He was in the days of His flesh, but rather in the hearts of all Christian people who love Him. But too often the procession fails to halt because it does not realise or does not hear the voice of Jesus in their midst crying "Bring him to Me." We are too content to deal with only surface needs by our thoughts of pity and of charity and leave it at that.

The story of the healing of Bartimaeus was, of course, not the only work of healing that Jesus did when He was upon earth. It is as well for us to realise that the Gospel records of the life of our blessed Lord are simply full of His healing mercies, and were we to take them all out, our record of His life would be a poor, emaciated thing indeed. Everywhere He went Jesus took the full Gospel, and this was proclaimed through Him, whether He was preaching or whether He was healing. His ministry was two-fold: He preached the Kingdom and healed the sick. The two went together, side by side and hand in hand. For too many centuries we have been content with only one half of His Gospel, namely the preaching of the Kingdom. Indeed, we have exalted this by changing the phrase to "preaching the gospel", whereas the proclamation of the Gospel is really the preaching of the Kingdom and the healing of the sick. The two must go together. They are integral to the whole Gospel.

Jesus came to break down the walls of our prison and to set us free in spirit, mind and body. His concern was for the whole man and not simply for the rescuing of our souls from the powers of evil. Every part of us He loved. When He began His earthly ministry and wished to proclaim what He was sent by the Father to do, He was handed the roll of the prophet Isaiah and selected from it one particular passage. That passage, which was to denote the whole character of His Gospel, reads as follows:

"The Spirit of the Lord is upon me because He has anointed me to preach good tidings to the poor, He has sent me to proclaim release to the captives and recovery of sight to the blind, to set at liberty them that are bruised, to proclaim the acceptable year of the Lord."

He came to set us free from the powers of evil which were let loose into the world at the time of our "fall". In our pride we thought we could do without God and, ever since, we have been caught in the prison of our own selfish desires. However hard mankind tried to be good and to reach up to God, mankind could never succeed; but, after long preparation, God sent forth His Son, born of a woman, born under the law, to redeem them that were under the law. His own Son He sent, the express image of Himself, because if man could never be good enough to climb up out of his own prison, He would have to come down into it. Only He could bring salvation.

As we consider this story of Bartimaeus, we need not, however, think of it simply as something which happened long ago and which could not happen again, for, thank God, Jesus is not dead, He is risen and is always alive and working today through the Church. He is the same yesterday, today and for ever, and His powers have never ceased. His Gospel is as alive today as ever it was, and His Gospel today is still two-fold: He sends us forth in His own name and in His own risen power to preach the Kingdom and heal the sick, to release men and women from their prison and to bring them by His grace to wholeness of life. Jesus loved to use the phrase, "Thy faith hath made thee whole." This word "whole" is a very significant one and it reminds us that He was concerned with every part of our being. He knows that the soul cannot be separated from

the mind and from the body; that if we are hurt in any part
of ourselves, then the whole of us suffers. So today His
Gospel is addressed to every part of our being, and as we
respond to Him in love and faith He will take that which
we have to offer to Him and use it in the furtherance of
His Kingdom in our own mortal lives here and now. This
is the good news.

We are not concerned with any kind of healing which is
not connected with the Gospel. What we are concerned
with is the bringing in of the full power of our Saviour
Jesus Christ into the total lives of men and women in
spirit, mind and body. True healing is that which is an
expression of our Lord's Kingdom, of our Lord's having
overcome the powers of evil which afflict us, just as
in the same way the preaching of the Kingdom will always
bring in its train the healing of our beings.

Some of us may already from time to time have felt the
healing touch of Jesus in our own lives. It may be that
some of us have had experience of this His power in a
remarkable way, but for most of us this has been an
experience of which we have not been able to talk and
share with others because, although very real to us, it may
not have sounded to be of much worth when related and
put into words. Most of us have known something of the
meaning of the words in that famous hymn:

> "The healing of His seamless dress
>  Is by our beds of pain,
> We touch Him in life's throng and press
>  And we are whole again."

Let us all try to discover something of the experience
which Bartimaeus was so privileged to enjoy. We all of us
have our individual needs, some more than others, but not
one of us can say with honesty that we have no need of
Him and His healing blessings. Let us be prepared to
listen for His coming. Let us be prepared to respond to
His presence in our midst and call out, with Bartimaeus,
for His divine help. If we really do that earnestly and with

all the love that we have in our hearts for Him, we can be sure that He will not simply pass us by. Nor will He be concerned only with our outer and surface needs.

As we call to Him, He will hear that need in our voice which marks our sincerity, our hope and our faith. He will halt in His tracks and command us to be brought into His presence. Then, with Bartimaeus, we can open to Him only our hearts and souls, knowing that He will see them clearly and with His great compassion. His and His only can be the words speaking to us of our healing. At that moment, on coming to Him and laying bare our souls and hearts before Him, let us release ourselves from the fears and the resentments and the jealousies and all the other things which belong to the kingdom of darkness and which now act as a barrier to His incoming grace and to His ability to use us as fully as we might be used in His service. It is as we feel His healing touch upon us that we shall be enabled to join ourselves to His company and to follow Him in the Way.

## 8

# WHERE PRAYER BEGINS

WHERE DO WE begin when we think about the meaning of prayer? I think that the easiest way to begin is simply to think of it as a conversation, a conversation that we hold with God and that God holds with us. To use the word "conversation" ordinarily is simply to think of the spoken words that pass between friends when they meet.

There are various levels of conversation. There is that somewhat surface level which passes for conversation between folk when they meet for the first time at a party: there is the much deeper level that exists between an old couple sitting at the fireside one winter's evening, though hardly a word has passed between them. It is this deeper level that we are aiming at. It is something much fuller than the conversation at the level of the spoken word. It is the unseen traffic of the heart that passes between two souls who are perfectly at home with one another. So, when we talk about prayer being a conversation with God, it is not just the spoken word that matters, the expression of our thoughts; rather is it the movement of the spirit as we reach out to find Him.

But if prayer begins with our holding conversation with God there is really, also, a time before that beginning. For, before we could hold conversation with God, He was there already. We can come to Him and hold conversation with Him only because He first was ready to hold conversation with us. He is, and always was, more ready to hear than we to pray. He is always waiting for us to turn to Him. He wants to do so much more for us in this life than we are ready and prepared to receive. So, if prayer begins with the idea of our turning to Him, remember that this could not be so were He not already waiting.

Think, for a moment, of the greatest Master of prayer the world has ever known, Jesus Himself. He would spend long hours in prayer and we can be sure that He was not just saying: "Father, please do this for me. Please do that for someone else." More likely He was listening to what His Father wanted to say to Him and was giving time to receive what the *Father wanted to give Him.*

When two people meet who are already "in tune" with one another they can easily talk together. But, even then, the words they speak do not matter very much. They enjoy a deeper level of conversation. They are, in any case, constantly in each other's thoughts. They are sensitive (even though "separated") to each other's vibrations. When they meet, therefore, and speak with each other they are only adding something to what already exists. The hug that you give to someone you love only adds something to what was there, all the time. So, when Jesus went apart to pray, He was only adding something to what was always there. His conversation with the Father never really stopped. It was continuous. While confronted by sick folk, when talking to the multitudes, while suffering on the Cross, His converse with the Father was continuous.

That is why prayer is to the Christian life what breath is to the body. You go on breathing all through the day and all through the night. Whether you are conscious of breathing or not, it goes on just the same. It is part of you.

There are times, of course, when you feel the need to take a few deep breaths. These times correspond to the times when you consciously enter into prayer. Don't think, therefore, that you ought to aim at two per cent or ten per cent of your day in prayer. Aim at spending a hundred per cent of your day. Then, the ten minutes or half an hour that you definitely set aside each day for prayer will be as natural and as needful as anything could possibly be.

"The time of business," Brother Lawrence said, "does not with me differ from the time of prayer; and in the noise and clatter of my kitchen, while several persons are at the same time calling for different things, I possess God in as great tranquility as if I were upon my knees at the Blessed Sacrament."

Brother Lawrence used to "practise the presence of God" all day through. In doing that he was following his Master. Jesus was always aware of His Father's presence. His whole life was lived in continuing conversation with God.

We, too, can develop a continuous awareness of God's presence. For He is always at work about us and in us. In Him we live and move and have our being. That is truth. To be aware of it is, after all, only to be aware of what already is! The development of a continuous awareness of God, His presence and His guiding, means that our minds, at least from the level which is just below our active consciousness and downwards, is always attuned to Him. This awareness may be likened to the awareness we have to the ticking of a clock in our sitting room. We may be thinking and talking of other things and as long as the clock goes on ticking, so to speak, all is right and well. But if it suddenly stops we notice it. We are impelled to get it going again. So with our life of prayer! It is really a part of us, all the day through.

## 9

# THE MEANING OF WORDS

WORDS, WORDS, WORDS! What do they mean? To one person a particular word means much — more, perhaps, than any word could ever hope to convey. To another, that same word means hardly anything at all. This is a common difficulty. We all experience it. Jesus did, and He was the most perfect conversationist who ever lived.

"To what shall I liken the kingdom of heaven?" He asked, time and time again. "It is like . . .", "It is like . . .". For Him, though, this business of conveying to others what was in His mind, was infinitely more difficult than for any other. No set of earthly words could ever convey the vision that He had.

We are only His followers, or trying to be, yet we know a little of this difficulty, too. Take the great words of religion like Salvation, Redemption, Reconciliation and so on. What do they mean? Ask one person and he will tell you one thing. Ask another and it will be different.

Salvation has to do not only with the salvation of an individual soul; it has to do also with the salvation of his whole being, mind and body, too, and with his whole environment. His relationships cannot be left out — with other people, with his daily job, with the world of nature.

And the word salvation also means healing. Whether you translate "The prayer of faith shall save . . ." or "The prayer of faith shall heal . . .", it means the same. Jesus went about healing the sick. The saving power that goes out from Him is exactly the same as the healing power.

So salvation is a big word, far bigger than many folk seem to suggest it means. We are all of us only at the beginning of what it is all about. Only One could see it clearly — right to the edges. Healing, too, therefore, is a mighty big word. It is not just a curing of a particular ailment. It can turn a person upside down. Christian healing can be shattering to a person who experiences it.

Many of those who tell us what has happened to them during the process of their healing do so with wondering eyes. Something has happened to them beyond their ability to express but they do convey the impression that they have been lifted by the vision of holy things. The actual ailment for which they sought healing is usually forgotten at the time. It is only afterwards that they realise it has gone, or is fast going.

Redemption, also, is a word that can mean little or much. H. W. Workman, one of the pioneers in the healing movement, often used this word. He wrote at least two books about it. It ties up with the redemptive work of God over and through His whole creation. St Paul catches a vision of its meaning when he writes the eighth chapter of Romans. "The whole creation groans and travails in pain together until now . . . waiting . . . waiting for the revealing of the sons of God." All the things of this creation are caught up in God's whole scheme and pattern of redemption. The world beyond is touched by it.

Every healing, every saving, has to do with it. A foretaste, an outreach breaking through from eternal perfection into the midst of things as they are. Breaking through the consequences of Adam's fall and redeeming by the power of God's second Adam, even Jesus. Redemption has to do with matter as well as spirit. It is vastly more than just a thing of the soul.

The healing ministry fills out the meaning of so many of our great words. Without the integration of this ministry into our total ministry most of these words seem thin and unworthy of the part they play in Christian theology.

## 10

## HAVING ALL SUFFICIENCY

THE FATHER'S gifts are always sufficient.

Writing to the Corinthians, St Paul twice speaks about this. First, he says, "Not that we are sufficient of ourselves, to account anything as of ourselves; but our sufficiency is of God" (2 Cor: 3,5). And later, "God is able to make all grace abound unto you that ye, having always all sufficiency in everything, may abound unto every good work."

I think of some of those dear friends who live or have lived by such unfailing promises as these. Some have passed into the fuller life. Those in this world live day by day and moment by moment attuned to Him and His ever-surrounding and never-ceasing bounty. He really does supply their need. They always have sufficiency.

Folk are so slow to learn this great secret. Yet Jesus always assured us it should be so. "Why be anxious?" He said. He spoke of the lily of the field and of the common hedge sparrow. "Seek ye first the kingdom and all these things shall be added unto you."

> "Said the robin to the sparrow,
> I should really like to know
> Why these funny human beings
> Rush about and worry so.
>
> Said the sparrow to the robin,
> I think that it must be
> That they have no heavenly Father
> Such as cares for you and me."

The disciples were worried because the three-days long crowds were hungry and far from home. Jesus said, "Give ye them to eat." "Not a hundred pennyworth of bread is sufficient," they replied. But Jesus took what was offered to Him, broke it and blessed it, and it became more than sufficient.

St Paul, like so many, learned this truth the hard way. Brought up strictly as all good Pharisees were, he learned to be self-sufficient, until this self-sufficiency was broken on the Damascus Road! "Why kick against the pricks?" the Divine voice asked. St Paul learned to sink self and to look to God. He never lacked after that. "My grace is sufficient for thee."

Remember David when he had lost everything, home, position, friends — driven out into the wilderness. Nothing and no-one to comfort him, to turn to in his need. Sitting on a hillside and looking across the valley he saw a shepherd with his sheep. Something stirred inside him. He began to think with a new mind. "The Lord is my shepherd; I shall not want." Although he had lost his home he knew now that he had found a larger one. The whole world was his because it was God's. "And I will dwell in the house of the Lord for ever."

## 11

## OUR DISTINCTIVE MINISTRY

WHILE THE CHURCH is accepting more and more that she has a responsibility for the healing of the sick, there is a certain amount of uncertainty about what that responsibility is.

There are three main lines of thought. The first can be seen in those who regard the whole sphere of traditional medicine as being the logical development and modern expression of the Lord's command to heal the sick. Most of our hospitals owe their origins to this belief. Some of our missionary magazines have, in the past, illustrated our Lord's command by showing photographs of doctors giving injections and nurses applying bandages.

The second can be seen in those who, more particularly, regard psychology as the thing. Thus, we get the remark of the parson who, in effect, says: "Yes, I do accept that the Church has her ministry of healing, therefore I must attend classes in psychology and discover as much as I can about what the psychiatrist does." In its extreme form it sees the Lord as having performed His works of healing through His extraordinary insight into psychological method.

There is good in both these lines of thought. No one with an ounce of Christian compassion can fail to see that. For our God stands behind and works through all channels of healing.

But however good they are and however much these lines are blessed and used of God they are not distinctively the Church's ministry of healing, nor can they completely satisfy our Lord's command to "Go, preach the kingdom and heal the sick." They may be baptised of the Christian Church, blessed and used in Christ's service, but they may also be similarly baptised by any other religion.

Which brings us to the third main line of thought. This is to see the Church's ministry of healing as being inseparably bound up with the Lord's work of salvation, with His own victory over all the powers of evil, with His training of the first apostles and with His command to go forth in His name to proclaim the gospel by preaching the kingdom and healing the sick.

While the two others are good, this is essential. While the two others are commended by the humanitarian conscience, this is commanded by the Lord. The ministry of healing which is distinctive of the Christian Church is integral to her very Gospel.

It is a matter of grace and not simply of the consecration of natural law. True, it fulfils law. But it is not bound by it. It goes beyond, and that is precisely what makes it a matter of grace. To us who are committed as Christian people to the Gospel it is a matter of *"By grace* ye are saved," or *"by grace* ye are healed."

His healing works were signs of a new order which absorbed and superseded law. They were expressions of a new Kingdom. They were to do with His whole work of making atonement. The healing with which our ministry is concerned flows from Him by grace. They could not be, had Christ not come.

When, therefore, we consider these three main lines of thought it is vital that we get them into their right order and into their right relationships with one another. To use the language of the examination room, the healing work which is distinctive of the Church's divinely commissioned ministry is compulsory for every ordained minister or priest of the Church while a knowledge of psychology and of general medical practice is optional.

## 12

## HIS HANDS AND HIS SIDE

HOW MUCH we all wish we could be in the Upper Room! How much we could wish this were the first Easter Day! How much we could wish we had actually experienced with our eyes these actual happenings! To have seen Jesus coming and standing there, breaking through the closed inner doors created by our fears; to hear Him say to us *twice,* "Peace be unto you," to give us this commission on the evening of our return home: "As the Father hath sent Me, even so send I you;" to receive from Him His Holy breath, giving us His Holy Spirit to take back with us, going back as different people because now, with authority, we can say to a sin-sick world "Your sins are forgiven!". How much we could all wish that this chapel in which we now worship were indeed that Upper Room! Yet you don't need me to add that this can be that Upper Room even here. We are gathered in His Presence. He is here, the same risen Lord who came to His first disciples. He is among us!

We know that He is risen, don't we? It is because He is risen that everything that we have experienced in our lives, in Him and for Him, makes sense. And yet, for some reason or another, the place in this particular passage which seems to compel my attention most this evening is that verse in the middle, "He showed unto them His hands and His side."

We think much of the healing power of the risen Christ. Let us think for a few minutes of the healing power of the risen but *crucified* Christ, because it is with hands pierced and side thrust with a spear that He is in heaven still. Other texts come flooding into the mind. There is the whole of Chapter 53 of Isaiah, "With His stripes we are healed", and so on. There is the great verse in St. John: "God so loved the world that He gave His only begotten Son." He doesn't just stoop out of heaven, however graciously it might be, to put His healing hand upon our lives, as though from a distance with kindly compassion, but He has been among us as our very Brother in the flesh, and what we have known of suffering, He has known too — and known it more deeply.

So I think the first thing about His healing is *He understands* and that, surely, is the beginning of all healing. Whatever you have to give to Him, He understands. He "stands under". After that comes the beginning of the pouring in of the realisation of His great love, "God so loved the world that He gave . . . that we might have everlasting life." This is the eternal, ceaseless outpouring of God's own life, not just everlasting minute after minute, hour after hour, year after year. This is a quality of life, *abundant* life.

I would like to illustrate all of this by a true story that shows how healing streams pour out from the very Cross of Christ. It concerns the time when I was chaplain of a mental hospital. While going round the wards one day I found a youngish man in a very bad state, and whatever treatment had been applied was unsuccessful. When I talked to him it was difficult to understand his replies because the tip of his tongue had been cut, also because he was a Greek who could speak but little English. He did talk with me, however, and I very soon realised that he really *didn't want to get well.* As he told me his story, the only thing I could say to him was "Well, I know Somebody who can help, and if you come to the Chapel you will find Him there." He was a Greek Orthodox and had not realised he could come to the Church of England Chapel but I told him that so long as anybody was here at the hospital he was welcome in that Chapel. He had a nickname among the people in the ward; they called him

"Napoleon". Napoleon had one or two habits of the Greek Orthodox which were new to me; one was that he wanted to kiss my hand every time we met! (We managed to restrict that one to Sundays only!) He wanted to stand for the prayers instead of kneeling or sitting — kneeling and sitting are quite modern, standing is a much older practice of the Christian at prayer and this is still observed in the Greek Orthodox Church. This was his story: He was a man of noble family in Greece and a leader in the Greek patriots. He was captured by the Nazis and put to very severe torture. But this young man refused to divulge the information the enemy sought. After they had finished torturing him they then brought his family in front of him and one by one they put them to death for him to watch, and the very final thing was that they cut his tongue and pushed him into a tiny little prison.

Some strange chance-happening enabled his friends to smuggle him out, not only from the prison but also from the country. They got him to England and brought him to this hospital. Poor Napoleon did not want to get well. There was nothing to get well for! He had experienced the depths of suffering and everything he had valued in life had gone! But he began to come to Chapel.

I don't know what it was that the Lord used, whether it was the prayers, the addresses, or whether it was a very lovely, rather large alabaster crucifix set over the altar. I am not particularly happy about alabaster and marble crucifixes, but this was a particularly beautiful one and did convey our Lord's understanding, His sympathy, His suffering. One could see, in that strange alchemy which changes human personality, something happened within Napoleon.

It seemed as though he was saying within himself, "No man can really get underneath, deep enough for me. I am down here at the bottom, no living human person can. But this figure on the Cross, this Jesus! He knows, He understands." One could see a new light coming into

Napoleon's eyes, and gradually — it took some three to six months — his healing happened. This was not a matter of ECT or drugs or anything of that kind, but the risen Christ showing to Napoleon His hands and His side. And so, one happy morning, we bade farewell to Napoleon, and back he went to Athens to begin life anew with the Master.

This Jesus, when He comes to us in a Healing Service, is One Who understands, Who knows our own difficulties, our personal difficulties, our difficulties with the parish, with the congregation, in our family, in our community. He knows, He understands. Yet He is so great in power. He overcame even death. Our Brother, and our Lord, He is risen and ascended.

So we *can* say "This is the upper room." He comes in to us and says "Peace be unto you.". He then breathes on us and sends us forth in His name. In breathing upon us, giving us His Holy Spirit, we somehow become temples of His Spirit, so that He is in us as we go back home. If through our hearts and conversation, through the reaching forth of our hands, healing comes into the community into which we are going it is He who is giving it. We are simply channels, by His wonderful grace and mercy. So praise be to the Lord who is in the midst with us, and praise Him that He shows to us His hands and His side.

## 13

## THE VICTORY THAT OVERCOMETH THE WORLD

*"Whatsoever is born of God overcometh the world and this is the victory that overcometh the world, even our faith"* (1 John 5:4)

WE KNOW that Jesus is the great Saviour and Healer and, for His part, is ready to give His blessings, but He asks us to have that faith in Him which can be the channel — or the pipeline — along which His blessings can flow. Remember how He moved about among the people and time and again, when He healed somebody, He said "Thy faith hath saved thee" or "Thy faith hath made thee whole." Of course it was God's power of healing and He it was who really healed but He wanted something of them too. He made that demand. Once, when He wanted to feed the multitude (He had the power to do it, but before He could do that He wanted our co-operation) He waited and waited until the little boy came forward with the five loaves and two fishes and at last He had got the something He was looking for — faith! And so He wants to bring us His blessings, whatever they may be, but He asks of us *our* part.

So faith is a kind of a pipeline along which flows, as in a channel, His blessings to each one of us according to our particular need and according to what He Himself wants to do and whatever He Himself wants to give us. "This is the victory that overcometh the world, even our faith."

Faith is a quality which is common to every man. Every man can put his faith wherever he likes. He can connect up his pipeline of faith, so to speak, to any particular set of resources. There are very many men who pin their faith on their bank balance! That, to them, is going to see them through life, and woe betide them if that particular set of resources cracks up! Perhaps when we are ill we go to a doctor. The doctor wants us to put our faith in him. He needs that faith. It is something we can supply and along that line he can work.

We can put our faith on to any kind of thing. Some things are good, some things are indifferent, and some are just plain bad. But it is a quality that is given us and it reaches its highest purpose (and the real purpose for which we are given it) when we connect it with God Himself, because there the resources are limitless and eternal. So, all those people who came to Jesus for healing, put their faith in Him, and along that particular line His powers were let loose into them and He was able to say, "Thy faith hath made thee whole." Faith, wherever we come across it in the Bible, of course, means faith in God, faith in Jesus, and it is this overcoming faith that finds its true destiny when it is put in Him.

Jesus warned us that in the world we should have tribulation — tribulation of different kinds in which we become involved because of the world's "fall" – whether in sin or sickness. But, "Be not afraid", He added, "I have overcome the world." Healing resources, then, begin in One who has actually lived among us and shown and demonstrated that His power does overcome.

We see Him in the wilderness being confronted by Satan and being tempted to reveal Himself in wrong ways as the Messiah, which He had to grapple with and battle with and eventually overcome. We see Him among the people, being confronted by demands from early morning to late at night, so that He had not so much as anywhere to lay His head — but always He overcame. We see Him set upon by His enemies, being taken by them into the courtyard, we see Him nailed at last to the Cross, and always He is the victor who overcomes every possible situation.

He is indeed the supreme victor, having within Him the limitless resources of God, and these are what He wants to let loose into our world and into our particular lives.

He is the same yesterday, today and forever. When we see Him in the wilderness, see Him among the people, see Him set upon by His enemies, see Him nailed to the Cross and see Him rise victorious, we see Him as He is today and it is this same Jesus into whose Presence we come.

We look to Him, setting our faith upon Him. He will never let us down. Other things may let us down — our bank balance and all the rest of it — but not He. He never cracks. We can take to Him our illnesses, or the illnesses of our friends, we can take to Him any particular problem that we have, any great difficulty; we can take to Him our fears, our resentments, our bitternesses, and all the other things which this world has done to us, knowing that He is the Victor who overcomes, because if our faith is in Him we have opened a pipeline for the limitless resources of Jesus, Son of God, Saviour and Healer, who Himself has indeed overcome the world, and we find that our faith channels into our beings the fruits of that great victory of His.

## 14

## THE AFTER-EASTER CHURCH

THE GREAT Forty Days of the Christian Year are still upon us. Let us enjoy every moment of them. They make up the most important period in our calendar and one longs for the Church to give them their due accord. So much is made of the earlier forty days of Lent. Extra services are arranged, Passion Plays and Oratorios are carefully rehearsed and produced, Christian folk pull up their socks in the matter of their own loyalties and obediences.

The climax is reached when Good Friday and Easter come. Then everybody goes on holiday: "The strife is o'er, the battle won." The rest is just so much aftermath...

What a pity! What a loss!

The message of the early Church was: "*Christ is risen!*". That is still the real message of the Church today. It was, and still is, a message of victory and power. Its implications are tremendous. We've hardly begun to live them out. Our Blessed Lord forever holds out to us gifts that are hardly ever noticed, let alone claimed and acted upon. Too many Christian folk are still basing their lives on a Christian philosophy instead of on solid facts of faith issuing from a continuous experience of Christ Himself.

But there are signs, good signs, that things are changing. The Holy Spirit is renewing the heart of His Church. One sensed the beginnings of a revival some years ago. It is gaining strength and impetus all the time. The signs are many. One of them is the changed emphasis from personal piety to active obedience, from our needs to the Master's needs.

Two or three generations ago there was, for instance, much self-concern about the number of lumps of sugar we should put in our tea during Lent and there was much preaching whose aim was solely to bring home to us our depth of wickedness. How self-centred this was is anybody's guess. It isn't what we are like that really matters, it is what Christ is like and what He is calling us to do for Him — now! That is what matters.

So, in these great Forty Days from Easter to Ascension, and so on to Whitsun (the festival of the outpouring of the Holy Spirit on the Church) let us lose ourselves in His Kingdom and His Kingdom's demands on us. That is the only thing that really matters. Our own personal piety, our own personal happiness, don't really matter compared with this. The only real purpose for our having been created is for God to use us.

Preach the Kingdom and heal the sick! Or, proclaim the Kingdom and so heal the sick, if you like to think of it that way. This is His command. This is the Gospel, the Good News. That's what we're here for, the purpose of our existence. To live in and to proclaim, by deed and word, the fact that He is risen, that He has overcome the powers of sin and sickness.

Healing is an affair of the kingdom, inseparable from it. His Easter victory has as much to do with sickness as with sin. The *whole* power of the enemy has been shattered by His resurrection, not just one half of it!

The Church must look at sickness as He looked and looks at it — as an enemy invader. Just as He looked at sin. He does not want us simply to accept sin and sickness without doing something to get rid of them — in His name. The parish priest or pastor or minister has a duty, under Christ, to his people when they are caught and held in bondage whether by sickness or by sin. The Lord wants them to be released from both. The Christian man or woman is also under obligation to the Lord to help by word and by prayer and so to seek their deliverance.

## 15

## THESE LATTER DAYS

*"Hark! A thrilling voice is sounding — Christ is nigh, it seems to say."*

THESE WORDS that we sing as every Advent comes along seem to me to be very relevant to this day and age. So many of the New Testament prophecies about the end of things are being fulfilled and, in the light of modern inventions and discoveries, make more sense to our generation than to any other.

The phrase, for instance, "distress of nations with perplexity." Only once in the whole of the New Testament does this word "perplexity" appear. It means "no way out" — like rats caught in a trap of their own devising. Could any former generation have caught the significance which it holds today?

To me, the rediscovery by the Church of her healing ministry, seems to find its significance when seen as an integral part of the unfolding of God's plan for His creation and especially for His Church. For though we say we are rediscovering our healing ministry, it is more true to say that it is the Holy Spirit Who is restoring it. In other words, this is a phenomenon *that is happening to us.* You and I are caught up in it. And not only we, but also our fellow-Christians throughout the world are being touched by this same movement of the Spirit. This "rediscovery" is universal. This phenomenon is happening to all the Churches throughout the world.

The Creeds that we recite are tabloid forms of the basic faith which has been handed down to us. But they also, as well as defining faith, present us with a quick picture, in historical sequence, of the unfolding plan of God for mankind. So, though every phrase in the Creeds has everlasting significance and speaks to every man in every age, there is a sense in which the third paragraph, "I believe in the Holy Ghost" has come especially alive today. It looks to the end and completion of things, to the perfecting of God's pattern for mankind. For this is the age of the Holy Spirit in a deeper sense than ever before.

One sees the marks of His activity everywhere, in the ecumenical sphere — where the broken parts of Christ's Body, the Church, are drawing together; in the quickened understanding of the Christian mind that God has called us apart — that while not of the world we are in the world with a job to do; in the new realisation of the Holy Communion as the central act of all our worship. The Parish and People Movement is one expression of that.

I believe that we have been brought into a greater degree of a sense of kinship with the primitive Church than has been in any generation of the Christian Church during all the intervening years.

Set all these against the world background of fierce ideological conflict, with all its terrifying complexities and possibilities in the political sphere, where there are wars and "rumours of wars" (is this another translation for "cold war"?) and remember that it, too, entered into an entirely new phase of history when the first atom bomb was dropped — and what have we?

We are not given to know the time or the end. When it comes it will come when least expected — as a thief in the night. But it makes sense to suppose that all these happenings fit, like a huge jigsaw puzzle, into one great and tremendous design. We are not given to see the design from God's "viewpoint"; we can see it only from our point of view. Like two sides of a coin.

From our point of view we see only the "signs" and we have to interpret them, under the inspiration of the Holy Spirit, as best we can. But even this we must do. The first disciples asked the Lord how we should know. He gave them indications but would not or could not (for He was truly and fully incarnate) give them the complete answer.

He reminded them about the signs of nature that herald the coming of the Spring. In this manner He said we must look for the signs of His "Coming". "When these things begin to come to pass, lift up your eyes... your redemption draws near."

Perhaps, from our side of the coin, going by what we are given to see, both in the spiritual and the natural spheres, it looks for instance, as though the chance triggering off of some frightful weapon, might be how it could appear to us. This, of course, is just on supposition; nothing more. But — we must watch. That is the thing that the Advent season lays upon us. Be watchful. Above all, know for sure that all is in God's hands and orderings.

In the meantime, there is another Advent message for us to welcome. It is in that same line I have quoted: "Hark! A thrilling voice is sounding — Christ is nigh!"

Of course, He is nigh. He always is. He is with us every day and in every passing moment. He is here with me as I look to Him to guide my thoughts; He is there with you — at your side, though unseen, as you sit there reading these words. He will be with you as you lay them down and wherever you go. To the end of the world — and beyond.

And — my word! — how much He presses Himself upon us in this, His work. How near He comes to us! And those blessed, shining ones with Him. The whole earth is indeed full of His Glory. Because He is always "nigh", this business of heaven and hell is to do with us here and now. Not just after we die. It has to do with our present acceptance or rejection of Him and with our acceptance or rejection of whatever He sends us.

His Coming is an endless process. He comes to us in every experience of life. Don't think that He comes only in the good, happy and uplifting experiences. He is there, behind, and coming through them all, "good" and "bad". He brings with Him His kingdom, destroying the powers that are destroying us, evoking that response within our beings that here and now makes Paradise a present reality.

## 16

# WORLD PEACE IS NOT OUR FINAL AIM!

WHAT ARE WE to say about the Church's place —
and every Christian's place in the world today? Though
we are not "of the world" we feel its pressure upon us far
too much to know that we cannot be otherwise than very
much "in it"!

You can't ignore the pressure of a neurotic person
when you've lived with him for some days; you can't
ignore the pressure of a neurotic world when you have to
live in it, as we do now, for year after year. Mr Macmillan
said that we have now got to learn to live with anxiety.
What a frightful thing to have to say! "The whole head is
sick and the whole heart faint!". Like petulant and
unmanageable children the nations wrangle with each
other from dawn to dusk, atom bombs are crackered off
in paranoid anger, the number of children who suffer
from leukaemia grows on our prayer lists, the weather
cycle reels like a drunk, even the plants in the garden do
strange things nowadays. World neurosis is all around.

First, I think, is to see in it signs which herald the Lord's
coming. That thought is never far from our conscious
minds. We are always watching. St. Peter, in his epistle,
bids us haste towards that Day (read the third chapter of
his second epistle — all of it). We say our creeds often. In
them we look forward to the culmination and completion
of God's great Plan for mankind. This thought is a
continuing source of rightful comfort for all who love the
Lord. But it should never be a mere form of escapism.
That is why there must be other reactions, too.

The second, surely, is to feel and share something of the
heartbreak of Christ in His tremendous love for all

mankind — not only for the righteous but for sinners also. Day by day fresh spears are thrust into His side. We think — and, in our mind's eye, we picture Him — on a hill overlooking the capital city: "O Jerusalem, Jerusalem, you who stone the prophets and them that are sent unto you, how often would I have gathered you as a hen gathereth her brood under her wings, but ye would not."

Then we remember that we, too, are far from spotless. We, too, both by our own, our very own, sinful thoughts and words and actions, as well as our day to day involvement in the sin of the whole family of mankind, add to His sufferings. We need a daily, an hourly, a continuous forgiveness as well as cleansing and renewal. Even with our brother Christians we lack complete fellowship through our lack of patience and unwillingness to share fully with them.

The next thought must be of His will being done — everywhere. It *will* be done, we need have no fear. What He wants (in point of fact He has made the world in such a way that we can say not only that He wants but that He also needs) is our will to work through. That is what prayer is about. It is not asserting our wills against His reluctance, it is not a matter of fashioning into prayerful-sounding phrases what we would like Him to do for us, it is not by thinking out how best to serve Him and so help to bring in His Kingdom and then asking Him to approve and bless our schemes (not even if we persuade ourselves they are for His glory), it is only by counting ourselves as dung (a New Testament word, this! — look at Philippians) and by submitting ourselves to obedience. Don't be afraid to let Him break you! Then you will know Him better and you will experience His peace, His joy. You will know the power of His Holy Spirit.

Prayers just for the peace of the world are not really what we are being called to aim at. It's something much deeper, much higher, infinitely more worthwhile. We are praying for the coming of God's Kingdom *and for the coming of the Day of the Lord.* Read the last two chapters of the Bible to get a picture of it. They include that lovely verse about the leaves of the tree being for the healing of the nations.

The kind of peace God wants for the earth is the kind of peace that the Christian already knows, the peace which does not originate in this world. It is Christ's peace. It is that peace which is a fruit of the Spirit. To pray for the peace of the world without being primarily mindful of these greater things is simply praying that the symptoms of the world's illness may be made easier to bear! What we have to pray for is the *healing* of the world. And the healing of the world begins when mankind breaks its own heart into the agelong heartbreak of Christ and accepts His will.

So, next, we pray for the outpouring of the Holy Spirit upon the nations of the earth. We pray that He will break down the pervading powers of evil (mankind cannot) and that He will turn the eyes of men to Himself. For, without the motivating energy of His Spirit, mankind cannot even begin to turn to Him and seek His will.

## 17

# THE OTHER FORTY DAYS

ONCE EVERY YEAR we come to the time when we hear the phrase "after Easter" quite a lot. The collect, epistle and gospel for the first, second or third Sunday after Easter is what the celebrant tells us as he reads the Holy Communion Service. Clergy and ministers take their "after Easter breather" and get back some of the energies they lost during the long forty-days stretch of lenten fast. It's all over now. The winning post has been reached. It is "after Easter" and we can rest.

Is this right? I often wonder about the emphasis we lay upon these days of Lent. Of the whole Christian year I suppose more work is concentrated into the season of Lent than any other season. There are always extra meetings and services to attend, special courses of sermons and addresses are prepared, special books written, promoted, urged upon us to read. Folk consider what they can give up, what they ought to start doing without for a change.

Now don't get me wrong. One would be a fool to say there is no place for discipline in the Christian year. Discipline is an essential part of Christian conduct and when this is centred on the very special theme of Lent concerning our Lord's self-giving for us all upon the Cross one can only bow one's head in humble assent.

No, what makes me wonder is not the importance we attach to Lent but its over-emphasis. It throws the Christian year out of balance. Ask anyone what the phrase "forty days" refers to and they will tell you, if they have any answer at all, the forty days of Lent. They won't all know how they're worked out — the Sundays will fox them — but they will be pretty sure that is what you mean.

But what about the other forty days? The forty days that *begin* at Easter? This is just as important a season as that which ends there. How many courses of sermons are prepared for this "after Easter" season — publicised so well — and how many books are urged upon us to read? What positive works are we urged to do, what discoveries to make of the meaning of this "after Easter" season?

We live in an "after Easter" world. That is the profoundest truth of all. This is a world that has been shaken to its roots by the resurrection of Jesus Christ from the dead. It is different a hundred times over, a thousand times over, from the world that existed before Christ came to overcome the powers of death and of evil.

Sometimes we talk about the pre-war world and the post-war world and say that things aren't the same any more. If there is any truth in that, how much more is there truth in the fact of this world having become completely changed on the first Easter morning! This is not simply to do with a date in the calendar, a passing event in history, a change brought about by the passing of time. It is cosmic. Its implications are terrific. The world is a transformed world because it is an "after Easter" world.

Christ is risen! We are risen! Get hold of this tremendous truth. Let it soak into you, let it penetrate into all your thinking — about death, about sickness, about temptation, about everything. Then ask yourself which of the forty days are the more important. Before Easter or after Easter?

So many good Christians — bless them — with all the devotion in the world, follow the via dolorosa to the foot of the Cross and there give themselves in utter devotion to the Saviour of all men. But they stop there. The magnificence of our Lord's suffering and self-oblation, His tremendous humility, are so over-powering that they want nothing more.

Yet, there before them is the *risen* Christ. "Go, tell His disciples He is risen." "See the place where the Lord lay." The risen Christ! That was the message of the early Church. Read the Acts of the Apostles and count all the references you can find. These first men and women of God's family were brimful of it all. He has overcome the world. "I am with you even to the end of the age."

Somehow, I feel sure that the rediscovery and use of the healing ministry of the Church is all bound up with this matter of emphases. So long as we restrict our gaze to the pre-Easter season, we shall be bogged down in something quite short of what Christ wants to give us, what He, the Lord of Life, wants us to do.

We can't by-pass the Cross. That isn't what I mean. We have to go to it, each one of us, sooner or later. And time and again we are brought back to it. But we were not meant to stay there for ever. We were meant to go to the Cross and through the Cross and find, on the other side, the victory. Then, having found the victory, we were meant to lay hold on it, to make it part and parcel of ourselves, our thoughts, our beliefs, our actions. We were meant to carry the fruits of the victory into the world and into the lives of others. To have our feet shod with the preparation of the gospel of peace — to go out as soldiers and carry out mopping-up operations because the battle has already been fought and the victory already won.

It is by the power of the risen Christ that men's lives are changed, that fevers are rebuked, sicknesses healed and demons thrown out. It is in the power of the risen Christ that we are called to go out preaching the Kingdom and healing the sick.

Let us look again at these two sets of forty days — one looking backwards from Easter and the other looking forwards and outwards — and ask ourselves which of the two ought to be over-emphasised (if, indeed, we have to *over*-emphasise either of them) if we are to capture again the victorious spirit of the early Church and to go out, in our own day and generation, bringing "His saving health unto all nations."

## 18

# THE WORLD OF MIRACLE

WHITSUNDAY, the festival of the Holy Spirit, is the birthday of the Church. Nearly two thousand years ago it happened. A miracle that has continued to this day. A continuing miracle that underlines the saying (first made, I believe, in the fourth century) that the Church is a divine institution because it would never have survived all this time if it were not.

The disciples were gathered together in their upper room — probably in the house of John Mark — and they were waiting expectantly. The forty days had gone by. The Lord had brought home to them the reality of His resurrection. He had appeared to them, not too much, not too little, but with that perfect care with which He had tended and nurtured them during the days of His flesh. Thomas had been more than assured, Peter had been restored. The Lord was risen indeed. They had all been convinced.

The period ended with His Ascension. Then had come a further period of waiting. A waiting for a miracle. No wonder, when at last it came, that it was accompanied by a rushing mighty wind and by tongues of flame!

The time of the disciples learning and following was over. They were apostles now — men on fire with a mission, transformed by the Holy Spirit. Suddenly they had to get out of the house and among the people they had previously feared. They had to tell them that this same Jesus Whom they had crucified was risen and alive. They were filled with an uncontrollable urge, caught up by a Power greater than they had ever known. They went forth and preached everywhere, the Lord working with them and confirming the Word with signs following.

So the Church was born. So the miracle was begun!

What are the consequences arising out of this for us today? First, to remember and always remember that the Church is a miracle now as much as it was then. It is holy. It is divine. It is born of the Holy Spirit at work in and through the hearts of men. Do you ever stop to realise the awful significance of those words you always use when you join in worship: "Take not Thy Holy Spirit from us"? Were the Holy Spirit to withdraw Himself from us then the Church would fold up overnight like a pack of cards.

The Holy Spirit makes the Church; not men, not clergy and ministers. All who bear office in the Church are called by the Holy Spirit. At the very most they are but channels. The Holy Spirit is what (or, rather, Who) is making the Church now, at this moment. He is breaking through this material plane while you sit reading these words. He is at work in His Church, now throughout the world, in your own country, in your own town. Miracle is all around you.

Secondly, it is precisely because the Church is born (and continuously reborn) in miracle that it is "natural" and logical to expect that which is in the nature of miracle to flow from her. The Lord confirms the Word with signs following. The twofold nature of her commission we have often spoken about. Preach the kingdom and heal the sick. The two go together. It is the Lord's own work. "As the Father hath sent me, even so send I you."

Sometimes, in our discussions, we consider the manner in which healing takes place. We consider the "make-up" of man, the interaction of spirit, mind and body. We understand, to some extent, that the spiritual or mental disposition of a person will affect his nervous structure, his glands, etc. We realise the harmful physical consequences of such mental causes as anxiety, resentment, stifled conscience, and so on.

We consider methods of prayer — contemplation, meditation, the entry into the silence — and we know something of the healing consequences that are set in motion through use of them.

Let us always be quite certain that when we do discuss these things we are discussing secondary matters, however interesting and helpful they may be. Let us always realise fully that the prime thing, the important thing we look for in all our healing work is miracle.

In this movement we are given the wonderful privilege of seeing men and women and boys and girls being brought to wholeness through the ministrations we are led to give them and through the intercessions that are offered for them. Never let us say that this person or that found healing *from* any of these methods. They found healing from only one Source — God Himself. It was miracle. God worked *through* them. It is the Lord's doing and it is marvellous in our eyes!

Thirdly, the disciples were waiting expectantly. What a real and important lesson is this! And how many long years it takes some good folk to understand and really to accept! We get a glimpse of heaven and we want it so badly that we can't wait! Or, we are so convinced that the kingdom of God can come for a certain person or for a certain set of circumstances in some particular way that we can't wait for God to perform it! This failure in the capacity of being able to wait — lovingly as well as expectantly — is often the very thing that stands in the way!

Put God first. Put the Holy Spirit first. Wait upon Him and give yourself and all your ideas in surrender to Him. Then leave it. Leave it entirely in His hands. He will perform what is best. In His time, which is always the best time! When this is done, when you have "let go and let God", you can be as certain as you like that forces are set in motion that are much more powerful than anything in this world. Beside them, the forces of the atom bomb are nothing. Only, wait on Him. Yes, leave it to Him. He will call you (or not) to do something perhaps, in His good time. You will know.

The disciples had been through it all. They had allowed the whole range of emotions from impatience to utter despondency to come up like barriers between them and God. One by one, the risen Christ removed them. They were, at last, ready and waiting, putting Him and His will first. This was the time for miracle. The Holy Spirit came in power.

This age in which we live is often called the age of the Holy Spirit. Well, perhaps it is. Certainly, wonderful things are happening.

There is a growing realisation of the Church as the Body of Christ, as a divine organism that is in the world but not of the world. Its sense of separateness is growing like that which was known and experienced by the early Church. Out of this sense many others follow — its fellowship with (and in) the communion of saints, its realisation of the Holy Communion as the central act of worship, its more serious approach to teaching in its proclamation of the Word, its anxiety over "easy" baptisms, and so on.

Then there is the drawing together of the Churches — the ecumenical urge. In the sphere of healing, this "pull" towards unity is tremendous.

We are living in wonderful days. Beyond the din of political strife, the crashes of atom-bombs and the roar of rockets flying into space, the mighty hand of God is at work in all our lives. Much, also, is happening in the spiritual world. The spiritual world has its own "laws". These break through into the natural world and appear, from the earthly vantage point, to be miracle. But they are precisely what we should expect to see happening about us for they flow from, and are the logical outcome of, a Church which herself is born and sustained in miracle.

## 19

## FELLOWSHIP DIVINE

WHEN A LOVED ONE dies your first feeling is of loss. There is a vacant space in your life. A prop has been taken away. This experience may be completely devastating at first, for not only has your loved one died but something inside you has also died with them. I was fourteen when my mother died. I was away at school. I was packed off by a prefect to see the headmaster in his study. He was gentleness itself and asked if I wanted to go home. I don't think I cried at the time. We don't usually, at first. That comes later when the full realisation of all that it means has time to seep into us. The headmaster must have been able to judge my feelings better than I could myself. He arranged my journey home immediately.

It was in the weeks that followed that I first experienced fellowship with the life beyond. I had been given a new bicycle and, like any other youngster, was thrilled both in possessing it and also in the fun it gave me riding along country lanes. It was here that my mother seemed to come to me again. She helped me push the machine along when my legs were getting tired. Yes, we had great fun together.

I have seen the passing of many loved ones in the long years since then and many folk have told me of their experiences, too. So, looking back, I am sure that the explanation of that experience is that our gracious Lord was allowing this fellowship to continue for a while out of the great love He has for all His children.

Although His resurrection appearances to His disciples cannot possibly be confined to this limited meaning, yet, at the same time, they do include it. He loved His disciples with a love greater than that of a mother for her child and His compassion for them in their loss was also a part, though only a part, of the reason why He came back to them. Yes, they did great things together.

There must be a period of mourning, a time for weeping. God wants us to have that. The road to resurrection leads through the Cross. It is wrong and harmful for a person to think he must stifle his tears when a loved one dies. True, he should try to keep his mourning (as he does his fasting) to his bedroom where God will share it in secret — and reward him openly. Beyond the mourning is gladness; beyond the loss is gain.

A clergyman whom I used to know very well told me how he went through this experience of mourning to gladness, through the Cross to the resurrection. He had just been appointed to a new and lovely living. He and his wife were very happily blessed with four (I think it was) young children. His was a very happy family. But, suddenly, as they were about to move, his wife died. It was devastating for him. As he and I were both newcomers to the diocese we naturally shared things together. If ever a man was under the Cross, he was. But, some years later, we met again. I had moved away and been invited back to the diocese to address the clergy at their annual retreat. He drove me to the station on the last morning in his new car. He was thrilled with it and told me that he felt that his wife was sharing it with him. Then he added something like this:

"You know, we shared her death together. I believe that when a man and his wife have the kind of love we had for each other they can't really experience the great things separately ever again. What happens to the one happens also to the other. When she died, I died, too. I felt within myself how she was feeling when she went on. There was a shadow of the Cross in it. We went through it together. Eventually, I came to share with her the unutterable joy of the resurrection. And this car? We couldn't afford one, then. The children had to come first. She shares my joy in it, now."

But, although there is still fellowship with our departed, there must be no selfish holding on to them. We have to let them go. This is as important for them as it is for us. To continue to hold on to them is to cloud our spirits in a prison of despair and remorse. Even if there is something we regret, something we wish we had not done to them, something that needs forgiveness — no matter what it may be — we still must let them go. If a cloud of remorse persists about us we shut them out still more. Remember, they are waking up in the world of light. Darkness and light don't mix. It is only when we learn to let them go that, strangely, they are able to come to us again. It is only as we release them into God that we can begin to enjoy their fellowship more fully.

And where do they go? Jesus spoke of Paradise. To the penitent thief upon the neighbouring Cross He said, "Today, you will be with me in Paradise." Paradise means park-land. It carries with it the picture of a beautiful garden. Time and again I have been present during the last hours of someone who is ready to go on. Often they have told me of a vision they have had during these hours. They have seen, they tell me, a most beautiful garden, full of loveliness. Certainly, the vision has brought them a real measure of the peace which is not of this world.

Is this, translated into human thought-forms and human language, what Paradise is like? It certainly seems so. And, sometimes, with this vision they have also been given a glimpse of the face of some dear one who passed on earlier, as though a welcome had already been prepared. Is that surprising when you think of all the preparations that we make here when a new baby is expected to be born into the world? Think of all the knitting and the sewing and the planning. Then think, in similar terms, of the preparations that are made beyond when one of our loved ones goes on to wake up in that more perfect world. That is another reason why it is selfish on our part and unhelpful to them if we do not thankfully let them go.

Jesus also spoke of "many mansions". The New English Bible translates the sentence in which this phrase occurs, "There are many dwelling-places in my Father's house; if it were not so I would have told you; for I am going there on purpose to prepare a place for you." This world is not the whole of the Father's house. It is only the first stage in it, the first of our dwelling-places. Beyond this stage is the stage of Paradise. And beyond Paradise is Heaven.

Often, too often, when people speak of this life and what lies beyond they speak as though this earthly life were the main thing and as though the life hereafter were but a kind of epilogue to it, as though what lies beyond were only a kind of added bonus. This is upside-down thinking. The real life is the life beyond. This life here is but the prologue.

The way to Paradise is through Christ. "Whither I go, ye know; and the way ye know," Jesus said. Thomas asked Him the way and Jesus replied, "I am the way." Later, He added, "I am the door." So, when we think of our loved ones in the fuller life, we must always think of them in their relationship to Him. Not just as unattached spirits in a strange world but still as persons — the same persons we knew them to be here — living now in His nearer presence. And by thinking of them as being in His presence we help them so to be. For this thinking is also a prayer.

It is important to think of them in their relationship to Christ also because such thinking will safeguard both them and us from psychic dangers. The psychic world is a world that lies between us and Christ's own world of Paradise. It is a kind of twilight world where there is as much evil as there is good, as much deceit as there is truth. Spiritualists dabble in this world. Avoid them. They may, in themselves, be perfectly sincere if they tell you they have a message from the other side for you. It is not their sincerity I doubt but the origin of their message. It was not for nothing that Christ called Satan "the great deceiver", that Peter warns us to be on the alert against the devil "who goes about like a roaring lion seeking whom he may devour." Evil spirits do exist. Not all angels are "angels of light".

Learn to think of your loved ones always, therefore, as being in the presence of Christ. Let them go to Him gladly. It will help them, also, to find their way to Him, the door of the sheepfold.

And if you feel you have a psychic door in your personality keep it guarded by the Cross of Christ. If you leave the door of your house open to the street, saints may walk in but so may thieves and murderers. Paradise is where Christ wants our loved ones to go. Don't spoil it for them by your selfishness. Paradise is a lovely world. Death does not exist there, nor crying, nor pain — for the first things are passed away. If they were lame here, they walk now; if they were blind, they see; if they were mentally afflicted they are free now and happy as they were unable to be happy here. For the Lord's preparation includes the wiping away of all tears.

Everything here that we know of loveliness — beauty, truth, goodness — is but a seeping through into this world of the loveliness that is there. We enjoy it partly; they enjoy it richly and to the full.

As we learn to discipline our lives so that we live them more and more in companionship with Christ, so does the world of Paradise become more open to us. We are allowed to see it more clearly. It is not entirely separate and apart from this world; rather, it interpenetrates it. It sheds a new light on the ordinary things. The whole earth becomes "full of His glory". And in the midst of this experience we begin to enjoy the communion of saints.

This is a phrase well known to Christian people. Most

of them regularly proclaim their belief in it but few of them really get to know what it can mean. They do not enjoy the blessings of its realities as they should. They live too much like lonely Christians or like members of a spiritual society based solely on earth.

The communion of saints is what Christ gives us. It is made possible by His Gospel, by His Cross and resurrection. It is in Him and through Him that we can have fellowship with all the shining ones in the life beyond. In times of prayer, when all our thanksgivings and petitions and confessions and surrenderings have been made, we can silently enter into this shining world about us. At these times, the veil becomes very thin. We can find rest in it. We can love them in it and let them love us. At this stage in our times of prayer we can really have communion with the world of Paradise. It is full of light, beauty and happiness. And our loved ones are glad that we are enjoying it with them.

Jesus, their Lord and ours, says, "Abide in Me, and I in you." It will be as you wait on Him — quietly, gladly, without rushing — and abide in Him, that you will be experiencing and enjoying the communion of saints.

Sometimes, too, you will be conscious of their helping or guiding hand. But it won't ever come if you seek it. You will suddenly realise that they are there — perhaps when you are lost in the enjoyment of some beautfiul experience or caught up in an act of worship or Christian service, or perhaps when clouds are around you and you really are desperately in need of help. Many of my friends have known this. I certainly have done — many times. And I always thank our blessed Lord for the help He allows them to give, for the fellowship He has made possible. It is as though they want to share with us something of the fuller vision they have themselves and perhaps also to say thank-you for having let them go.

## 20

# FAITH

IS FAITH necessary for healing? Yes, it is. Time and time again Jesus said, "Thy faith hath saved thee." It was a quality that had to be there if His work was to be effective. The degree of faith present, or partially present, had a determining effect on what was to follow. "According to your faith be it done unto you."

This quality of faith was to be seen usually in those who came to Him for healing, but sometimes it was to be seen in those who represented them. When the four friends carried the man sick of the palsy into His presence it was *their* faith that He used. " . . . and Jesus, seeing their faith, said unto the man sick of the palsy . . ." On other occasions He used the faith of someone who was closely related to the sick one. There was a woman of Canaan who besought His help for her daughter, the father who asked Jesus to heal his epileptic son, the centurion who came asking Him to heal his servant. Faith was present in all those vitally concerned with the one who was actually sick.

Faith is a quality that all of us have. It is a gift of God, and, like all gifts, can be used rightly or wrongly. There are many things in which men put their faith. In money, in a cause, in a person. All of us have to put our faith in the milkman, the train driver and the service of thousands of people we don't know but who keep our lives going day by day. Without faith, life is impossible.

Yet the highest use of this gift and the chief reason why we are given it is that we may ultimately come to put our faith in the living God.

The writer of the Epistle to the Hebrews defines faith as

the "substance of things hoped for" (Hebrews 12:1). A Harley Street doctor told me many years ago that he often pondered on the meaning of this text. It fascinated and intrigued him. It prompted him to think of faith as a kind of living energy, as a creatively healing force in itself.

I feel that there is much in this. There is undoubtedly a creative energy at work where faith is present. Faith is the substance which becomes transmuted into visible reality. Perhaps what Einstein has taught us about the interchangeability of energy and matter has a significant relevance here.

I often think that a doctor does far more good, unconsciously, for his patients along the line of faith than along the line of the medicaments that he prescribes. A patient who has great faith in his doctor will benefit from his help far, far more than the patient who has little faith in him, even though the needs of the patients and the medicaments prescribed are the same! And, again, if the doctor has real faith himself in the particular drug he is prescribing for his patient it will have a more potent effect than one which he is not himself sure about. Something is conveyed from doctor to patient which is often as important as the drug he gives and sometimes even more important.

The picture that always comes to my mind when thinking about the thing we call faith, is that of the feeding of the five thousand. Jesus wanted to feed the multitude. The words placed in brackets in the Authorised version are very important. "He himself knew what he would do." Jesus's will was that the multitude be fed. That is what He wanted. But that this might become possible, the right conditions had to be created first.

He told the disciples to feed them. They couldn't. They thought of all sorts of reasons why they couldn't. They told Jesus why it could not be done. But Jesus stood firm. He waited . . . Eventually a little lad came along. "Look," he said, "I've got these few loaves and fishes.

Use them!" The conditions, now, were just right. There was faith in the little lad's heart. This was what was needed. Picture the little boy, if you can — no wonder Jesus spoke of the faith of a little child — as, his eyes shining, he brought his poor little gift forward.

And Jesus took the loaves and gave thanks . . . He could now do what, all along, He had wanted to do.

What Jesus wants to do for each one of us is so very much more than we have even begun to realise. "He is able to do exceedingly abundantly above all that we ask or think." But are the conditions right? What is the measure of our faith to receive? It isn't that He does not want us to get better, it isn't that His will to heal us today is less than it was when He was upon earth. He is the same yesterday, today and forever. But have we the faith to receive?

It is no good trying to simulate faith, no good trying to concentrate all our mind into a feeling of faith. Sometimes a sufferer will come and say, "I am full of faith that this is going to heal me." They have already decided what the outcome of the ministration is going to be! But what they are implying doesn't really work out that way. It all depends on what it is they have faith in. Is it perhaps a faith in their own capacity of faith that they think is the be-all and end-all of the matter? Is it faith in the act of the laying-on-of-hands itself that they have in mind? This matter has its importance, of course, but there's much more to it than that!

The kind of faith that Jesus can use is not a manufactured faith. It isn't something that originates in the feelings or emotions. The kind of faith that Jesus can use has to be evoked. It is a response to Him and to His will. It is like a tiny spark within, which only a vision of Him can fan into flame. In other words, it is a consequence of something greater than itself. It is something that happens within oneself when one suddenly sees Him and knows what He can do.

Those who came to Jesus when He was among us on earth had already seen or heard Him. He made a tremendous impact on them. He, by what He was and did, evoked in them the capacity of faith that He needed to work the works of Him that sent Him. There was one place where He could do no mighty work because of its lack of faith. That was in his own village. Because it knew Him simply as a carpenter's son it could not recognise Him for what He truly was.

Insight is closely related to faith. All through His ministry Jesus insisted that those who recognised His true identity should keep it secret. People must find Him for themselves.

When, at the close of His Galilean ministry and before going on to Jerusalem, He took His disciples apart and led them way up north to Caesarea Philippi, He turned to them and questioned them about this very thing. He asked them whom men thought He was. Eventually, when they had replied to this question, He said, "And whom do you say that I am?" Suddenly, Peter saw Him clearly. "You are the Messiah," he burst out, "the Son of God"!

To see Christ clearly — that is the great thing! To see Him and, therefore, to know what He can do. That is how faith comes about. The kind of faith that Jesus can use for our healing. Though faith is essential to healing work it isn't faith that heals. What heals us is the power of the living Christ. Faith taps that power, it doesn't provide it.

The woman who pressed through the crowd to touch the hem of His garment was soon to discover this. Virtue went out of Him. Yet, her faith was essential. As the disciples remarked, many people were touching Jesus at the time. They were all around Him. But there were faith and intention in her particular touch. Her faith tapped His power and provided the channel along which His healing virtue could flow.

What it amounts to, in the end, is that what really matters is our vision of the Christ Himself. That vision will determine the extent and quality of our faith. We must keep Him always in our minds and hearts, we must learn more about Him from our Bibles and in our prayers — accepting with humility the challenge that this inevitably brings. We must "practice His presence" day by day and always be malleable in His hands. This is how faith is born. This is how faith grows.

## 21

## ALWAYS GIVE THANKS

"BE CAREFUL for nothing; but in everything by prayer and supplication with thanksgiving let your requests be made known unto God" (Phil. 4:6).

Thanksgiving is a very important part of prayer. We don't give half enough time to thanksgiving. Perhaps it is because there is still far too much of the worldly mind in us that is always wanting, never satisfied however much we have. Like a child always wanting another toy.

We need to "count our blessings" daily. And learn to appreciate and to enjoy what we already have far more than we do. Sometimes prayer goes "dead" on us simply because we forget to list our causes for thanksgiving.

A deaconess was telling of a difficult time in her early days. Spiritual things seemed to be drying up. She was going through a dark patch. She went to her Spiritual adviser and told him about it. She said she found she couldn't pray. She was going through the motions as best she could but nothing seemed to help. Her counsellor wisely told her to stop trying to pray for a while. He asked her, instead, to spend ten minutes each day in listing things for which she could give thanks. She went back to him from time to time and it was not till two years had gone by that she returned to her full prayer life. But ever since, and that was many years ago, she has been grateful for those two years of nothing but "thanks, thanks, thanks." You can imagine the permanent effect of this experience on her life.

When Jesus's life was overclouded with threatened evil and all forces of the enemy were gathered together for His destruction "He took bread *and gave thanks.*"

St. Paul was always giving thanks. When he prayed for his friends it was always "with thanksgiving". He says to the Philippians, "I thank my God upon every remembrance of you, always making my supplication for you all with joy." He speaks about the kind of inner life which every Christian can enjoy in Christ, like this: "singing and making melody in your heart to the Lord, giving thanks for all things."

God has given us so many good things and He wants to give us so much more. Why, then, come to Him as though we had to implore Him to be good to us? Why imagine that we have to wrestle His gifts from His grasp? Think again and give thanks. When you ask Him for something, ask Him thankfully.

Thanks be to Thee, my Lord Jesus Christ, for all the benefits Thou hast won for me.

## 22

## ABOUT EXORCISM

TO LOTS of people this subject evokes all kinds of queer images of strange goings-on in haunted houses and so forth. And the folk who dabble in it are thought to be a little weird. Maybe some of them are. This makes me feel I'm sticking my neck out in writing about the subject. But many of our readers — particularly clergy and ministers — have been pressing me to do this for some time — so here goes!

Let's try and get the matter in proper perspective first. Back of all sin and all sickness lies "the fall". In the midst of the fall is Satan, the "prince of this world", the deceiver. Our life is not simply a matter of living through three score and ten years here on earth, earning a living, making a career, eating, drinking and sleeping. It has to do with eternal things, "spiritual" things, with "psychic" things, with wrestling not simply with flesh and blood but with all the powers of darkness. This we realise more and more as we live "in Christ".

All sin and all sickness is, then, diabolical in origin. Sickness (of soul, mind or body) is an enemy invader, something to be recognised as against the perfect will of God. Jesus is quite clear about this. To Him, sickness is a thing to be got rid of. Not, for Him, is sickness ever seen to be a thing sent by His Father to teach us the value of suffering, deeper understanding, compassion, and all the other things that Graeco-Roman philosophies have taught us. He gets rid of it and, in getting rid of it, tells us what the Father "thinks" about it.

His word to the Pharisees, "If I, by the finger of God, cast out devils, no doubt the kingdom of God is come upon you", explains the attitude that lies behind all His healing work.

Exorcism, the casting out of devils, is therefore to be seen as having something to do with the very heart of our Gospel and not as something weird that only strange fellows dabble in. It has to do with our life "in the kingdom", with our wrestlings against the powers of darkness. It has to do with our awareness to the great realities in which our lives here upon earth are set. It has especially to do with prayer.

Our total gospel is two-fold: "Preach the kingdom and heal the sick."

And the healing aspect has three expressions: "Heal the sick, cleanse the lepers, cast out devils." These are closely related and often intertwine; though, in practice, and in accordance with the sufferer's individual need, one is more dominant than the others.

"Cast out devils." Exorcism. This particular aspect, this particular expression of the Kingdom's power itself covers a wide range.

It begins, at one end of the scale so to speak, with "rebuking", and goes on to exorcism of an obsession and then to exorcism of a possession, at the other end.

It begins with rebuking. This is usually an attitude in the heart of the ministrant when confronted by an illness that is destroying a person's life. It is a response evoked in him to an enemy invader, to something of ultimately diabolical origin which is despoiling God's creation. (Incidentally, all medical work is ultimately based on this hypothesis, too.)

The attitude of rebuking may, or may not, be expressed in words. It is primarily an attitude of the heart, born of a Christ-desire to see the sufferer liberated from the thing that has become bound to him. Too often, Christian compassion takes the wrong turn at this point. It will seek, instead, to bring the kind of comfort to a sufferer that will enable him to "bear his sufferings". True, this is bound to be so long as the illness is still there but not in such a way as to "bind" the illness to the sufferer indefinitely while being vaguely hopeful that the doctor will soon rid him of it!

Jesus condoned illness no more than he condoned sin. Both were of diabolic origin, manifestations of that Kingdom which had the prince of this world as its head. He could be moved with compassionate anger if confronted by any doubt about the Divine willingness to heal. His reply to the leper, "I will, be thou clean" was of this sort. The leper had said, "If Thou wilt, Thou canst . . ."

Taken to see Simon's wife's mother, right at the beginning of His ministry, He rebuked the fever. He recognised it as an enemy invader. He did not simply put soothing hands on her brow. To speak only words of comfort would have been to accept the illness and to have helped bind it to her.

A young teenage girl, suffering from a skin disease, was brought to me by her mother. Ever since her vaccination at six months of age she had suffered so. She had to wear cotton next her skin, cotton gloves, a shawl covering most of her face. Every morning her mother had had to sweep the fallen skin from her bed. As this young girl talked with me I discovered that, despite her dreadful trouble, she taught the little ones in her Sunday School. So I said to her, "Well, you don't need me to tell you what Jesus would do about this thing if we took it to Him, do you?". She knelt at the communion rail while we offered it all to our blessed Lord. Then, in His name, I turned to her and rebuked the illness. Then I laid on hands and gave her the blessing.

That night, it seemed as though the trouble got much worse and in the morning her mother had to sweep away more fallen skin than usual. But, after some forty-eight hours, it became obvious that the skin was clearing and a new baby-fresh skin was beginning to take over. We met again a fortnight later. The healing was almost complete. There was no shawl now and, as she knelt at the communion rail again, I saw she had a head of beautiful fair hair and the thought struck me: "This is how the Father intended it to be." I felt His "smile" upon her as I laid on hands again in the Divine name. Afterwards, as we said goodbye, her mother said, "Did you notice her hair? I have told her through the years that I felt it could be lovely. It was so, even when she was very tiny. Now she knows for herself."

Often, when giving the laying-on-of-hands, one has been moved to rebuke the illness — sometimes silently from one's heart and sometimes aloud. And usually, when pain is present, one has rebuked this. It usually responds and gives way. I often think that when a child runs to his mother and says, "Mummy, please kiss it better" something far more significant is happening than is commonly realised. Love, expressed through a touch, will usually "melt" pain. Love infused by the power and authority of the Christ is more powerful still.

Why, oh why, is not this rebuking and this infilling of the Divine love done more often? The body of Christ has hands as well as lips. Why must they hang so hopelessly, so often, when His healing love and compassion are bursting to be expressed? Hands are given to convey as well as to receive. The power of Christ's kingdom must not be restricted to the voice alone. The lips can do much but so can the hands and the eyes! Our whole being must proclaim His Being and His ways!

From this attitude of rebuking we progress up the scale, so to speak, and come next to the rebuking and casting out of an obsessive illness — one that has clung to the sufferer and from which the sufferer can, by himself, find no escape.

Homosexuality and lesbianism, alcoholism, depression, some forms of epilepsy, and many others come to one's mind at this point. Quite often the sufferer will speak of his struggles with the powers of darkness. To a doctor he probably wouldn't mention this, nor ought he to do. That is not the doctor's province. But to a priest or minister who has met these things before and whose whole life is concerned with the things of the unseen he will more readily do so.

Unlike the doctor, we must enter into an empathetic relationship with the sufferer. This is a matter of sharing, entering into, his sufferings as though they were one's own. After all, is not this the Christ-way? There is no other! But while sharing it with them, one is still, please God, "in Christ".

By the end of the interview and before the following ministration, both of you see that this thing, this illness, is a "dark" thing, an enemy, and that the risen Christ has power over it, to cast it out.

So, you minister to the sufferer. Christ's love and compassion are strong within and about you and in His name you rebuke the thing (it may be "this spirit of dark depression") and command it to come out of the sufferer. You address it direct, you are firm with it and speak strongly to it in the name of Jesus. Three times you do this, slightly changing the words you use each time you address it. I usually make the sign of the Cross over the sufferer's head while doing this. Then, turn to the sufferer himself, lay your hands on his head and speak the words of healing that Christ will put into your heart. Sometimes you will find yourself calling on the assistance of the holy angels and of all the powers of heaven to give the sufferer protection from further attacks and you claim for him the inward strengthening of the Holy Spirit.

Afterwards, you will feel a measure of the exhaustion that the sufferer himself is feeling, so you tell him to rest for an hour or two and to take the rest of the day quietly. You tell him also to come to the next celebration of the Holy Commuinion to partake of the blessed Sacrament, the medicine for all our ills. You might also tell him to use

the sign of the Cross over himself if any further attacks
threaten. And you tell him that the most powerful prayer
in all Christendom is simply that of putting the name of
Jesus on one's lips.

These things you do. But, and this is important, you do
them only because the Holy Spirit is leading you, guiding
you, *making* you use them. If this motivation is not there,
you do whatever else He bids you do. Only one thing is
really needful — *Christ's love in your heart.* There are as
many ways as there are ministrants of giving expression to
His healing love. He wants to use you as you are, and not
as someone else is!

A year or two ago I had the privilege of sharing with a
doctor a ministration of this kind. It was near the
conclusion of a mission when he and I were together on
the platform of a large hall with a big and crowded
meeting in which many folk who couldn't find a seat had
to stand at the back and along each wall at the sides. The
atmosphere was pretty electric. First, he spoke and then I
did. After the chairman had said a closing prayer a lot of
folk pressed round us asking to hear more and to ask
advice on various personal problems. There was little
time to deal with any of them. One of these was a
Presbyterian minister who had brought a young man of
his congregation who suffered from epilepsy. I felt it was
too difficult to give real help or advice in a case like this,
especially in that somewhat crowded and noisy scene.
Had I been able to help I would have liked to ask a whole
lot of questions first. So I suggested he got in touch with a
local clergyman whom I knew well and who, I felt sure,
would be only too ready to help.

A little while later the doctor came across to me. He is
an eminent surgeon and well-known in his part of the
country. He, too, had been crowded around with a mass
of people asking his help and advice. "We've got a job to
do here", he said, "and we can't put it off! I've just been
having a long talk with a Presbyterian minister who's

travelled over fifty miles to this meeting to get help for a young man of his congregation. We've just got to do something before we go and you know what it is that has to be done!"

The crowd was beginning to disperse but the hall was still somewhat noisy. The vicar of a church just down the road came to our help. "Use my church," he said, "I'll go and unlock the side-door into the chapel."

The young man knelt at the communion rail with the vicar and his minister just behind him, also kneeling. The doctor and I were in the sanctuary. On the way over we had chatted about this illness and about this particular case. Before coming over to me in the hall he had asked both the minister and the young man various questions, mostly of a medical character, before becoming quite convinced that this was exactly what had to be done.

After a time of prayer, I said the words of exorcism while the doctor stood by me. Then, together, we laid our hands on him. The power of the risen Christ to heal was present in strong measure in that otherwise empty church that night.

We now move up the scale from exorcism of an obsession to exorcism of a possession. And here we find possession of two kinds, the first more common by far than the second. The first is possession by an unclean or evil spirit and the second, possession by a discarnate (human, earthbound) spirit.

When thinking about this area I am most profoundly grateful for having a certain amount of knowledge of mental illnesses. Since my medical student days the psychiatric field of medicine has always been that which has appealed most to me. And, in particular, I tremendously value the four years I spent as resident chaplain to St Andrew's Hospital, Northampton — one of our leading psychiatric hospitals. I mention this because although it isn't at all essential for a parson to have medical knowledge before exercising his own given authority in the Church's ministry of healing (indeed, a short course of psychology can be more hindering, even, than helpful!) but because I do think that before using exorcism in this particular range some check ought to be made concerning the trouble from which the patient is suffering. Some classifications of mental disorder can look like demon possession, but they aren't, and a lot of unnecessary harm can be done if this ministration is used. If there is any doubt at all, don't use it. In any case, always remember that the greatest therapy of all is LOVE — love born of compassionate sharing with the sufferers, love that will make you sit with them and hold their hands, love that doesn't necessarily have to be spoken.

Not very often — but too often, nevertheless — one has seen young enthusiasts for the Lord and His Kingdom bursting impetuously to rid a poor sufferer of his "possessing demons" and only having the effect of stirring "them" up more than ever!

During the interview preceding whatever ministration one is called to give, one goes pretty deeply into the sufferer's troubles — particularly into the kind of person he really is. One feels within oneself something of his struggles and his hopes, his emotional responses to situations, his loves, his hates, his bitternesses, his frustrations and resentments, the mental and the physical pain he suffers, and so on. Occasionally, there comes one for whom no explanation of his troubles can be given except that here is a person possessed of an evil spirit.

A young woman who had suffered various illnesses, mental and physical, told me that she didn't want to come to see me and had been brought by a friend. Her first words were, "You can't help me. Nobody can. I sold myself to the devil two years ago." I asked her to tell me about it. There had been trouble she told me, all through her life, and then came a harsh blow which made her very bitter. It was then, she said, she had done this thing. I need not go into the whole story. After the ministration she walked about like somebody in a dream. Two or three days later she asked me what had happened. Like most of these people, her memory of the actual exorcism was so vague as hardly to be recalled at all. She only knew that something bad had passed away, that life was supremely good and that heaven was near. She is all right now, going regularly to her church at home and wanting to be confirmed.

It is strange that the exorcism itself is not remembered — or at least only very vaguely. It only seems as though they have emerged out of a bad dream, out of a dark night and into the sunshine.

Finally, we come to possession by a discarnate spirit. This is very, very rare indeed — and, even then, one wonders!

There was an old lady who had been a religious. During the war she was a matron of a nursing-home run by her community. A young man, a scoffer, had been brought in — following Dunkirk. He said he was an atheist and teased her about her religion. He was discharged and she lost sight of him. But she felt she ought to pray for that young man and she did. His name was David. A year or two later she felt a strange presence about her and this feeling increased during her prayer-time and at the Holy Communion. She came to know that it was David (though it was not till long afterwards that she made enquiries about him and discovered that he had been killed at Tobruk at about the time she first began to feel his presence). At first, she didn't mind. She thought she was helping him and he seemed grateful. He had so much to learn.

This was not a case for casting out an evil spirit. I asked her many questions and eventually decided to accept that it was indeed David. She showed no other symptoms that might have indicated mental trouble. The pragmatic approach seemed to be the only one possible.

We sat, side by side, at the back of our little chapel and

I talked through her, with David. David knew he ought to go on to paradise and be with Christ (David kept calling Him "the Shining One") but didn't seem to have the strength. Eventually he went and we said goodbye to him. The religious sighed deeply after he had gone. She wept, too. But she was released.

What the explanation was, I do not know. I could do nothing other than I did. Whether I interpreted it rightly or wrongly God was pleased to bless what was done.

Exorcism is only one small part of our total ministry, (which is perhaps just as well for it is somewhat exhausting!). It should be done *only by a priest or minister;* and it should, wherever possible, be preceded by holy unction for the protection of the sufferer's person.

Whenever it is used, it is essential that the ministrant watches for a possible recurrence of the trouble about three days later (sometimes three weeks, sometimes three months — it is strange how this number three comes into it). If it does, use the ministration again and remember to tell the spirit to go to that realm which God has appointed for all wicked spirits and to stay there and not return. The second ministration (if necessary) completes the exorcism and the sufferer must then be built up into the sacramental life of the Church. (It worried me the first time it happened and I was mightily comforted when, searching the Scriptures for an explanation, I re-read the bit about the spirit going out into dry places and then wanting to return).

How blessed are the Holy Scriptures! They tell us of the coming of the Christ the Blessed to overthrow the powers of darkness and to establish His Kingdom. They tell us of how He selected twelve from all His disciples to train them and prepare them to be His Spirit-filled body, they tell us of the power that is in the holy name of Jesus, and they record the promises He made that His church would go out into all the world ... and preach ... and heal. So many other books are written — theological, philosophical, psychological — and many of them help us. But sometimes they do tend to hide, rather than reveal, the true and mighty treasures of the Scriptures!